3FE

Find, Focus Establish the Fundamentals, Execute

The Tool for Motivational Empowerment

By
D.S. Brown

Copyright © 2021 D.S. Brown

All rights reserved. No part of this publication may be reproduced, distributed or transmitted in any form or by any means, including photocopying, recording, or other electronic or mechanical methods, without the prior written permission of the author.

Book design by Queekpub.com

TABLE OF CONTENTS

Introduction ii

Chapter 1: The Simplest of Methodologies 01

Chapter 2: 3FE in Pursuing an Education 07

Chapter 3: 3FE For Who You Want To Be 29

Chapter 4: Identifying 3FE in People 43

Chapter 5: 3FE On The Job 61

Chapter 6: Lock The Job 93

Chapter 7: 3FE For The Future Entrepreneur 107

Chapter 8: 3FE In Faith & Religion 117

Chapter 9: Social 3FE. 129

Chapter 10: Voting 3FE. 137

Closing 155

INTRODUCTION

And there came a day unlike any other, more urgent than all that had come before, when I could no longer stand against the onslaught of withering pressure, nagging details that wore me down to the bone, boiling anger and angst that flourished in this world of unrecognized worth, engendering self-doubt and bottomless depression, impending failure that threatened to claim me mind, body, and soul.

When all seemed bleak and at an end, I turned and reached out with a striving hand. I knew not what I was reaching for. I expected nothing as I reached in desperation. Expectations can set one up for disappointment, but like the person who knows the end is just around the corner I grasped, thinking it was in vain, but reached and grasped nonetheless, hoping for that miracle that is at the heart of human nature. When all seems bleak, won't someone, something come and save me?

I reached, reached, and grasped. In the mental center of my metaphorical hand I felt something real and solid. I had grabbed hold of hope. I examined my find with inward mental vision and what I beheld was a tool, a tool I had developed months ago as part of another effort. It fairly leaped into my hand off of the shelf in my mental library. I looked at what I held with an appraising eye, and smiled. I knew it was my salvation, and that the answer always did reside within me. I only needed to find the courage to take hold of it, embrace it, and put it to good use.

How was that for grandiose?

I have a penchant for going over the top. It makes me smile. You fellow nerds and Stan Lee fans out there will recognize my opening as a play on words from the Avengers, the seminal Marvel Comics superhero group. As I'm writing this the Mighty Avengers has made its debut in this summer of 2012, and it was absolutely amazing! I was totally immersed in this created world of superheroes, and imminently pleased to see some of my favorite fantasy characters brought to life on the big screen behaving like ordinary people, but with extraordinary powers. They bickered, they argued, they fought. But when it mattered they came together as a team, a team focused with discerning critical thinking skills, using their minds as much as their super powers in order to handle together a world threatening problem that no one hero could handle alone. Oh yes, to win the day they needed the power of teamwork.

So, what do superheroes have to do with solving personal problems?

In the real world, not much of course. However, in our imaginations women and men who can fly, lift buildings and handle dastardly foes partnering with ordinary men dressed in bat costumes doing things well beyond the ordinary … well, that's quite motivating. It's uplifting. It's even fun.

I've considered this book in relation to superheroes because my goal is to empower each and every one of you to such a degree that you feel like superheroes, that you possess such a tool that makes you feel capable of facing any challenge, overcoming any obstacle, feeling strong enough in your approach to a problem that achieving success is a foregone conclusion, and that even though the possibility of failure is real, it is not the focus of your concern.

You are now possessed of a tool that motivates and empowers. It gives you what you need to move yourself aggressively forward, to wade deep into the waters of problems, issues, great concerns, and on any given day that may be quite unlike any other, you are ready to hold fast and use the tool for motivational empowerment, and achieve critical success.

My goal is to make you believe, truly believe that with the application of the right tools within a critical thinker's mindset you can accomplish whatever goal you set for yourself. Understand that within this personal mandate you establish for yourself the sincere application of critical thinking skills, which will prevent you from seeking an objective that is downright impossible, or ludicrous at best.

Regarding the typical, and what many of us call asinine (the things that far too many people focus on), can you sing? Can you rap? Can you throw a round ball through a hoop? Can you run fast? Can you appear in front of a camera and with firm conviction convince others that you are actually an entirely different person in a fictional story? In other words, are you destined to be an actor, singer/rapper, or athlete? Yes, utilizing critical thinking skills in a manner that highlights your abilities and focuses them on discerning the truth will either lead you further down this path, or as is appropriate for the majority of you, it will guide you to your true purpose so that you may put down the fantastical nonsensical fantasy and truly embrace your own personal truth, and realize your dream. Are you a powerful teacher waiting to emerge? Are you a merchant with the gift to sale? Are you a problem solver, a dentist, a pediatrician, an electrician, a carpenter, a plumber? What are you?

You will know limits. You will understand your capabilities. You will know what is outside of you, and be able to discern what must be internalized within you. You will clearly recognize what's already inside, those special gifts that have been provided to you and you alone, identifying you as someone unique and special. You will know that through truly understanding yourself, how you relate to others, and how this all comes together with a sincere understanding of what drives you, what you're passionate about. You will know what you were meant to achieve, and that with the mindset and appropriate tools you can achieve just about anything. This will be so very uplifting and motivating as to make you feel you are truly flying; and that with the right plan, you can succeed. In order to establish this plan for success you will be armed with the tool for motivational empowerment, 3FE. And through 3FE you will achieve Critical Success. And what is Critical

Success? It is the planned achievement of something urgent and essential, utilizing careful planning and judgment for the express purpose of attaining personal prosperity. So, let us begin.

Chapter 1

The Simplest of Methodologies

The problem is before you. You are filled with uncertainty. You don't know what to do next. This is not a good feeling at all. Each and every last one of us has felt this way at some point in our lives. Some of us have felt supremely confident on some occasions, absolutely certain we understand everything that's transpiring and what exactly has to be done in order to solve the problem.

Unfortunately, far too many of us claim to have never had this feeling, that we are always awash in a sea of confusion and dismay, trapped in a box labeled failure, with no sign of the light, no direction, no hint of success, and thus absolutely no motivation. I want you to say a number and two letters. I want you to internalize this number and two letters. Whenever you begin to feel yourself slipping and the doom is impending, I want this number and two letters to leap to your mind. In the face of the question, this is always your answer.

I don't know what to do. What do I do? I know … I will use … **3FE!**

The tool for motivational empowerment is represented by this number and two letters. They open the doorway to the utilization of the most simplistic of critical thinking tools. By utilizing this method you can look directly at the problem, clearly define the problem to the best of your ability no matter the complexity, and with enthusiasm clearly define a course of action that will lead to a successful resolution.

This is the power of **3FE**.

The so-called tool for motivational empowerment is named thus for a few very simple reasons. One, it is indeed a tool. As you confront a problem you can readily put this tool in your mental hand and engage in problem-solving, and I do mean aggressive problem solving. As we work through this book together you will learn how 3FE can be utilized to breakdown the most intractable, difficult, complex problems, and manage them effectively, either working them towards full resolution, or getting the issue appropriately staged in order to utilize a more stringent methodology that will better resolve the problem.

Recognize that the actual activity of approaching problem-solving in such a manner is powerfully motivating. How, you ask? Imagine starting from a point of nothing and by using a tool gaining knowledge bit-by-bit over time, gaining understanding bit-by-bit over time. With each little step you feel like you've gained more ground, like you've gained on your problem, beating it into submission, understanding it implicitly and thereby working towards eventually defeating it. This is you ... winning (no celebrity puns please). Still, winning is indeed powerfully motivating, and by feeling strongly motivated, you feel inherently empowered, responsible and accountable, and most assuredly quite capable of resolving the problem at hand. 3FE ... indeed, the tool for motivational empowerment.

BUT, WHAT IS 3FE?

In order to understand the tool in greater depth let's break it down into its constituent components. 3FE stands for Find, Focus, establish the Fundamentals, and Execute. The acronym eases the task of remembering the tool and what it stands for. You must Find, which in terms of problem solving means Find as much information about the situation as you possibly can. If the problem is easy this may be a quick exercise. If it is difficult this will take more time. If it is complex then you must Find out which smaller parts make up the larger problem and Find also what makes up those smaller parts. You must engage your mind in a brainstorming session either alone or with your team, and Find the details. Find all the details that matter. Do your research.

Finding the information that comprises the problem is first. Then, once you've looked at the details you've gathered it's time to Focus. This is not an easy thing and requires the utmost attention. As we go through the motions of our everyday activities we often find it very difficult to focus appropriately. However, focus is at the very crux, the core of the 3FE methodology. Without it, you cannot move forward and achieve critical success.

Look at the first piece of information you have. Study it. Add additional details, dig deeper. Look for information that perhaps ties it to the other pieces of information you have. Do the same for the second piece of information, and for the third, as well as the fourth. As you focus on the information, the details will start to take on meaning. First, let's be clear, what you did in the Find phase was gather your data. Data is meaningless without clarity and understanding. With understanding data becomes information, something to be understood, it carries meaning. Your collection of data will start to carry meaning. You will be able to see patterns as you continue your Focus exercise. From the information a natural order of progression will arise. In terms of solving your problem you will start to see meaning and address one of the issues first. Then, you will seek to address the second issue. Then you will seek to address the third. Your Focus exercise will imply a certain order in which you will go about executing your tasks. This constitutes something important, and readily moves us into the next phase of the simplest methodology.

Once you've completed your Focus exercise you will move on to establishing your Fundamental plan. The basis of your plan will have been derived from the relationships and tasks you identified in your Focus phase. Now, you must work on solidifying the plan, advancing it as far as you can to the point of perfection for execution. Now, please understand the use of the word perfection here is relative. At no point during this entire exercise should you become lost in what is commonly called *analysis paralysis*. You must be wary and not get locked into continuing cycles of either research in the Finding or Focusing phase, or cycles of refinement in the executing the Fundamental plan phase. You'll never get to end of job, which means you'll never achieve critical success.

You should seek to perfect your plan to the point that you feel your objective is fully achievable having minimized the risk of failure to the best of your ability. This does not mean you will automatically succeed, and failure is impossible. Failure is our constant companion and always a possibility. However, by building the strongest plan you can and minimizing risk you have done the best you can with what you have, and now you're ready. Look at your plan. Examine the steps. Have you covered all your eventualities? Is your plan as clean as you can get it? Are the tasks lined up appropriately? Have you listed the resources required with each task? Have you clearly established your milestone dates? As you look at this plan does it clearly get you from A to B, A being where you started examining the problem and defining your objective, and B representing your problem solved and all activities ending with success? Does this plan look good enough to you to achieve critical success? If so, then you're ready.

The last part of the methodology requires consideration and should not be taken for granted. It implies simplicity just as the entire 3FE process implies simplicity, but do not short it of its due diligence. Even in the act of execution the possibility of failure looms. Ever heard the phrase, *failure to launch?* The last part of the methodology is indeed Execution, however as stated don't take it for granted. Once your plan is ready all you need do is pull the trigger and execute your fundamental plan. However, always remain critical thinking throughout. As you immediately embark on the first part of your plan be vigilant and thinking, watch to make sure your execution is clean and that no unforeseen circumstances crop up to derail your progress.

However, with due consideration I will say that at this point I would like for you to smile with the promise of what's to follow and PULL THE TRIGGER! Fire for affect! Run it & Gun it! You have a plan, now follow it! EXECUTE! EXECUTE! EXECUTE!

This, ladies and gentlemen is 3FE, the simplest of problem-solving methodologies, the motivational tool for personal empowerment. **FIND**, gather the data. Seek it. Leave no stone unturned. **FOCUS**, look at the gathered data with a discerning eye. Question the data. Construct relationships. Turn the data into meaningful information. Establish the **FUNDAMENTALS**, examine the information thoroughly, changing what is applicable to the situation into actionable steps. Build your plan. Finally, **EXECUTE**! Luck is nothing more than preparation colliding with emphasis at the intersection of fate and opportunity. Find the data. Focus on the data. Establish your Fundamental Plan. Then, Execute! Do your **3FE!**

Chapter 2

3FE In Pursuing an Education

This is without question the best place to begin in earnest. The tool for motivational empowerment is most applicable in the area of education. In fact, education is very much the core of all our endeavors, leveraged most effectively in order to achieve the best results.

First allow me to clarify what I mean by education before we get into the details. I firmly believe education is our foundation. A requisite education as we grow into adulthood is essential in providing a strong foundation for whatever activity we seek to engage in later in life. Still, even after we graduate from high school and college, or a trade school, or whatever next step we take, continuing our education is an absolute must.

As human beings we are designed to use the gifts we have been provided. We must exercise our minds just as much as we exercise our bodies. This means we must cultivate a life-long love of learning, of engaging the world around us, in continuing our education beyond the class-room and always being committed to learning, and learning more, and learning even more if we can, as an activity to be enjoyed throughout our lives.

Where does 3FE come into this personal mandate of education? As stated, it is the tool for motivational empowerment. It should aid you in completing the task of getting educated. It can be a boon to student, teacher, and parent. It can be utilized as an essential problem solving tool for any enterprising adult seeking to do more, and in order to do more you must learn more, you must further your education. 3FE is just the tool to help you do it.

However, let us begin at the beginning; or rather one of the beginnings, a very important one to be sure. Let's go over the usage of 3FE in the classroom. This is essential information be you a young student, parent of that student, or adult continuing your education in the classroom. Hopefully, if you're an adult student, your classroom challenges are different from the ones our children face. Still, the lesson from a general perspective remains very much applicable.

We are presented with a problem. The classroom is a place of learning. You are attempting to learn. You are not being successful. The teacher is challenging. The material is challenging. Everything is challenging and you find yourself facing failure. This is the problem to overcome and we must find a way to overcome it. We seek motivation. We seek empowerment. We reach for 3FE.

Pause …

The book is about the tool, and the effective utilization of the tool, but I would be remiss in getting started in this, the second chapter, without covering some old and comfortable ground. As we go deeper into this journey of using the tool for motivational empowerment, as we start our walk in that which is the foundation, education, I feel it is absolutely paramount that we consider what's core to the rule, what's core to this foundation, what's core to the necessary educational mandate.

In everything I write you will find this kernel, the seeds that drive my own personal mandate, that which I aspire to, will never fully achieve, and am far from being the best. I'm a life-long aspiring critical thinker. However, I'm just a man with hopes and dreams, just like anyone else. I'm not a powerhouse of philosophical thought. I don't maintain a lofty space of dominance in the field of intellectual debate. I have not cornered the market on logic and how it is effectively applied. What I have done is aspired to such things, setting goals that are both realistic and attainable. In all that I have done, or hope to do I have considered my limits as well as my capabilities.

In doing this, I make myself into a powerful aspiring critical thinker. I think and move with due consideration in all things, or at least I try. In doing this it is important to understand what critical thinking is and what is the critical thinker.

Like I said, it's old comfortable ground that needs to be covered again, and again. Repetition reinforces internalization and eases execution, where appropriately applicable. Take your time to consider that sentence if necessary. Find some friends and discuss it. Use your critical thinking skills to break it down and internalize my meaning by defining your own meaning, seeking to relate it to my own.

Critical thinking, what is it? As simply defined it is the act or practice of one that thinks with careful, exact evaluation, and judgment; indispensable, and essential cognition; to consider, anticipate a possible action as a result of careful analysis and evaluation.

How often do you do this?

I would hazard a guess that you don't do this as often as you would like. That's okay, that's what this all about. We want to increase our propensity towards leaning into critical cognition. It takes work. In order to become such a person you must do it over, and over again. You must exercise your mind in its rigor just like you exercise your body. In order to think better, you must work on thinking. I want you to commit now to becoming an aspiring critical thinker. It will aid you in being a better person all-around. Internalizing this desire and making it a mandate in your life is core to the effective utilization of the 3FE tool. And to put it quite simply, the two are inextricably intertwined. The good thing about it is if you seek to use the tool, you're thinking critically. The more effective you become at its use the better thinker you will become. And when utilizing the tool and exercising your mental chops as an aspiring critical thinker, it is always important to recall the Hallmark of the Critical Thinker:

The hallmark of a critical thinker is the sincere ability to internalize the perspectives of others, most especially when that perspective is diametrically, or even violently opposed to your own.

>How does this help us in using the tool?
>How does this help us become better thinkers?
>How does this help us in the classroom?
>How does this help us with our foundation?
>How does this help us improve ourselves?

The answers are quite simple but imminently illuminating. When using the tool you have to be able to look at as much of the data available on your issue as possible. This data may not be agreeable to you. However, it is still data, quantifiably it carries value. It exists, right wrong or indifferent. You must consider it. By considering wider possibilities you are increasing the value of the solutions you derive by using the tool.

You are taking into account more variables, considering more outcomes. You're doing this not only with facts, but opinions as well. And this is very important to consider as we enter into the classroom. Is there an opinion that you don't belong in this classroom? Is there an opinion that you lack the mental ability to succeed in this area of study? Is the generally accepted opinion that you will fail?

As stated, we must critically consider our limits as well as our capabilities. It is well and good to believe we can accomplish anything under the sun and moon. Anything we set our minds to is achievable; such an opinion is a powerful function of belief. This purposeful opinion is good for motivation, both for self, and for a given team. We consider the team because we can't do it all alone. Everyone needs help and everyone needs to consider their team when entering into an endeavor. However, for your part, for the thing you do with your skill alone, you must be able to think critically about your own innate gifts. Do you have a passion in this area? Are you truly capable of achieving the objective?

Here's the crux of the matter with due consideration. We must strive to always live our lives in a state of growing, ever learning, but we must also know when to quit a thing, or even not start a thing. This is the heart of knowing our limits as well as our capabilities. Don't misunderstand. This is not to counter the motivational advice that you can achieve, that you can do whatever you set your mind to. This advice quite simply asks that you set your mind to goals that you know are achievable, or even impossibly achievable due to some changeable circumstance. In other words, though the mountain may reach to the sky and everyone is telling you you'll never reach the top, you've thought about it, you know a way, you see it, and you know you can achieve it. YES YOU CAN!

Consider, do you have a passion for physics? Are you a lay engineer? If you are not, then you should not set a goal to try and build the world's first commercially viable fusion reactor. I want you to dream. I want you to stretch your imagination. You may very well start the world's next conglomerate. And make no mistake, you may be the person that does have the passion, skill, and drive to finally fuse atoms together in a controlled-reaction. However, the differentiating factor is that you have what it takes to be a physicist in the first place. You know your capabilities, as well as your limits. If you don't even understand what I just said about atoms, then don't waste your time on advanced physics courses. As a student, get what you have to get and then move on.

With due consideration, a focus on our foundation, and a core commitment to think critically in all that we do, we are ready to apply ourselves to utilizing 3FE: The Tool for Motivational Empowerment, in the classroom.

Some of you are good in the classroom. Some of you are absolutely brilliant. And some of you are horrible. Some of you are just plain horrible students, and you can't seem to find a way to make things better. You're the group I'm going to focus on. The brilliant students can take this information and aid others they see in the classroom that are struggling. Understand, aiding others enhances you as a human being and even increases your overall brilliance. You good students can use this information to strive for brilliance, and like the brilliant students enhance your good experience and turn it into a brilliant experience by using what you've learned to help others.

So, you students that are having problems, you students that are challenged in the classroom on a daily basis, you so-called horrible students, I want to ask you to do something for me. I would like for you to take a moment and delve deep into critical thinking and grab hold of honesty. I want you to be absolutely honest with yourself.

Why are you having problems in class?

You may be struggling for a variety of reasons, but in Finding how we can improve classroom performance, and thus education, we must identify the various reasons we're having problems in the first place. What is the problem? This is not a trite exercise. If the first thing that comes to mind is the teacher is awful, and it's not my fault, then you are not thinking critically. Let's take a really deep breath and consider the word honesty. I want you to be honest with yourself, and what's going on around you. The teacher may be a problem. The classroom may be a problem. Your books may be substandard. There may be too much disruption in the classroom. You may have a job that wears you out on a daily basis and you simply don't have the energy to focus in class. There are any number of reasons that may signify why you're struggling in school. Look closely at the problems you're experiencing. Think about them deeply. Grab hold of them tightly with the hand of your mind. Now, grab a piece of paper and a pen.

Slowly, carefully, with emphasis write down your problems on this piece of paper. Read them aloud. Now, read them again. Let the words settle.

Before we go any further I want something else to settle on your mind. I want you to understand the critical importance of reading and writing. Adding arithmetic to this tried and true old school approach to education gives you the truly fundamental foundation you require in order to build your intellect onward and upward. You must read. You must read. You must read. And you must write. You must write. You must write.

Writing, and rewriting an idea, issue, or point of interest reinforces that idea, issue, or point of interest in your mind. Rewriting will provide clarity and perhaps bring forth more thought, additional perspectives on the issue, different angles from which you may approach a problem, and thereby solve it.

Getting back to your piece of paper.

If you have one major problem with the classroom, let us proceed from there. If you wrote down several, I want you to focus on the problem that you consider to be the greatest. Which of your problems do you see as the most challenging? We'll work that problem and proceed from there.

Underneath your major problem I want you to answer the following questions about what's really bothering you in the classroom with regard to this problem. Remember, be honest:

- Who is the problem? Who is at the center of your issue? Is it you? Is it the teacher? Is it someone else in the class? Again …. is it you? Really, is it you?

- What is the problem? You're repeating what you already did here as part of your initial Find phase, writing down the problem. However, read the problem again, and see if you can't add any additional details over and beyond what you've already listed. What more can you think of that makes the issue more difficult to deal with?

- Where is the problem? Don't be silly and just write, *in this classroom.* Think critically about the question. Where is the true heart of the problem? Is it in the textbook or other course material? Is it in how the teacher gives you the information? Is it in you? Really, is it in you? Are you tired and can't concentrate because you spend too much time working at Big Bun's Beef & Burger so you can buy a silly overpriced pair of jeans and some hair weave? Or, must you work at the Beef & Burger to help support your family? Is this an uncomfortable truth? Answer yourself honestly. Where is your issue?

- When does the problem occur? Is it always in the class? Is that really where it starts? Perhaps it's when you're away from the class. Do you understand the material when you're in class, but can't make sense of it any other time of the day? Even better, is it only when you're tired? And if that's true, why are you tired? Still working hard at the fry station at Big Bun's Beef & Burger?

- Why is this issue a problem? All these truths will tie together once you've gathered all your facts. This simple analysis is you first step towards isolating the flaw that impedes the building of your educational foundation. You must ask yourself why this issue is truly a problem, and always be honest. What is going on in your mind, in your home, in your community, in your life, in your school, in your environment, that makes this an issue for you? Why is this issue causing you to have such a problem with your classes?

- How is this issue an issue? How has this problem become real for you personally? I want you to take time and study the problem from all angles. Ask yourself the How question. Analyze it deeply. How does the issue work? Think through the steps of the issue as it impacts you every day; and remember to keep it as simple as you can. Add on layers of complexity as you build your analysis. You can start as simply as this, *I open the book. I read the words. I listen to the teacher. I can't make what he says match what I'm reading. This doesn't make sense. I don't understand. I quit.*

At this point I think we should introduce you to the simple structure of the 3FE tool. It is nothing more than a collection of rectangles. Remember, at its core this is a tool for motivational empowerment. It is not meant to overwhelm, but rather bring ease to the problem-solving process, and by virtue of its methodology make you feel a great deal better about being able to solve the problems be they the simplest, requiring one use of the tool, to the more complex, requiring several iterations of 3FE analysis. Which, just to make it really simple, means that for complex problems you may need nothing more than a good pencil, several pieces of paper, and the ability to read, write, and draw a lot of boxes. How's that for simplicity? Like it? I know I do. Let's proceed.

3FE	Find ... Focus ... establish the Fundamentals ... Execute!!! **Issue:**
Find	Identify the issue. Find what it is. Open your eyes, ready your mind, set your attitude to full on positive and engage in true critical thinking. Question everything, and then write it down. Who ... What ...Where ...When ... Why ... How
Focus	Look closely at what you've found. Focus on it. These pieces of information aren't truly information yet. It's all just data. Dig into the details and clarify the bits and pieces of the data. Take note of the relationships between the bits of data. What additional details are there to consider?
Fundamentals	As the relationships between the data points becomes clear a path arises from the data, and things begin to make sense. When data has meaning, it becomes information. Information has value, and inherently can lend itself to a solution. This is the Fundamentals, the essential tasks that bind the information together into action steps that resolve the issue.
Execute	Because sometimes you need an execution plan. Maybe you're going to execute in phases. Maybe you'll execute in one fell swoop, all at once. However, you do it, do it with emphasis! **EXECUTE! EXECUTE! EXECUTE!**

The above is the essential tool. This is the simple framework into which you will build your 3FE analysis. Feel free to expand on it. Feel free to add additional rows and columns. Feel free to do with it what you will, so long as you remain true to the original mandate, the sincere utilization of critical thinking skills in a powerful effort to effectively utilize the tool to be motivated and empowered. From there it's yours, take it, seize it, claim what I offer as your right to use and achieve Critical Success.

Let's use the tool and complete the classroom analysis.

3FE	Find ... Focus ... establish the Fundamentals ... Execute!!! **ISSUE 1: Improving Classroom Performance**
Find	**Who:** I honestly think it's me a lot. I also don't think my teacher knows how to relate to me. I'm an immigrant minority and I think this is a problem for him. **What:** I've got a failing grade and I hate this class. The book is difficult to understand and I'm not able to get any help in making it understandable. My notes don't help, because I don't really know what the teacher is saying. He doesn't like repeating himself and reminds us of this all the time. **Where**: I have to keep a job to help my family. I work at Big Bun's Beef & Burger and it takes a lot of time and energy. Working and staying in school is extremely hard. **When:** This isn't a sometime problem. When I'm in class I'm not participating because I don't follow. When I'm at home I don't know what to do and how to do it in order to keep up. When I'm at work ... well, I'm working.

	Why: I think this is a problem because honestly, first I don't feel motivated. My English is good, better than some of my friends who were born here. Everything is just so hard. It's hard at home. It's hard at work. It's hard at school. It's just hard. **How:** It's always the same. Open the book. Listen to the teacher. It don't work. I don't connect. Everything feels heavy. I put my head down a lot. I go to sleep. I'm not the only one to do this though. If I don't understand, why should I pay attention?
Focus	**My Teacher & Me:** There are a lot of us immigrants in the classroom. I think he might need some help in relating to us. I don't know for sure. But if I'm honest, I think I resent having to work harder to understand. I think this should be easier. I think we should be able to understand each other. And he shouldn't be so boring. Sometimes, I think he acts like he doesn't care about us kids. He sounds the same all the time. He looks the same. He doesn't care. And I guess I don't care either. **Solution:** I want to care. I do want to get my education. I guess … I could talk to him. I've never had a conference with my teacher. My parents both work too hard to take the time to talk to him. I can try harder to stay awake. And then, there's Wilma. I remember Wilma offered to help tutor some of us. None of us took her up on the offer. She's really smart. I guess I could take her up on her offer. I know it would help. I've been really stubborn about things. I'll talk to the teacher, and Wilma.

Beef & Burger: I need to work, there's just no way around it. But my father told me my education is the number one priority for me. I've been kind of ignoring him because to me it's important to help the family. This has made us kinda angry at each other. I think I need to do things a little differently.

Solution: I can work with my manager to scale back my hours a bit. She's really nice and supportive. She might let me take study breaks during my shifts too. But first I have to learn how to study right in this course. That goes back to getting that help from Wilma.

Reading and Writing are hard: I have some problems with writing I know. I remember one of the admins saying there were two workshops a week at the school that would help all of us immigrants. I never followed-up on it. If I'm honest with myself I'll admit I need this.

Solution: I don't have a lot of free-time at all, but I will promise myself to go back and look into these workshops and figure out how to fit them into my schedule. I'm just tired of making bad grades. I've had enough.

Tired all the time: Okay, I work too much. I'm always tired.

Solution: I'm going to actually start planning my day with a To Do list so I can organize all my stuff throughout the day. I'm gonna try to go to sleep at a decent hour every night (this will be really hard).

I HATE SCHOOL: I would like to like school, but how?

Solution: I'm gonna read that poem Attitude by Charles Swindoll every morning before school. If I change my attitude and get enough rest, and do all the other things, maybe I won't feel this way.

Fundamentals	**Task 1:** I will schedule a meeting with my teacher and discuss my difficulties. My goal is to build a relationship of some kind with him as best as I can. I will let him know I am committed to getting a good grade.
	Task 2: I will ask Wilma to tutor me. I need the help.
	Task 3: I'll work with my Manager on my schedule at the Beef & Burger. She's always been very supportive.
	Task 4: I will sign up for those workshops on writing at school.
	Task 5: I will put together my daily To Do list and prioritize my daily activities.
	Task 6: I will read ATTITUDE by Charles Swindoll every morning before school.
Execute	I'm going to execute my Fundamental plan starting next Monday, October 17th.

And there you have it, a complete 3FE analysis for the classroom. To be sure, it's very simple, certainly with much to fill in, but it clearly defines intentions, provides energy, focus, direction, and leaves enough room for alteration and change as may be appropriate. It is just as it is meant to be … a start.

We utilized a particular analysis tool in order to clarify the Find phase. We added additional details in the Focus phase, which highlighted particular points about the core issue and even established some relationships among the different parts we detailed. With good focus we were able to clarify specific measures we could take to start resolving the problem. These specific measures were turned into *action steps* in the Fundamental phase. With a clearly defined plan in-hand we were able to establish a starting point, a date on which we would Execute. That is 3FE in action!

There are a few more additional points with regard to classroom performance that I would like for you to consider when conducting your 3FE analysis. Whatever your problem may be these core considerations are absolutely necessary in my opinion, in order to formulate your plan for achieving Critical Success in the classroom.

CLASSROOM TOOLS

1) COPY ANOTHER PERSON'S STYLE

Many of you may have heard the saying *imitation is the sincerest form of flattery*. It is indeed true. There is a difference between mocking someone, or copying their style for amusement, and copying them because the way they do something gets good results. If you ask that person for help in learning how they do what they do, they may even take the time to help you. In the classroom, as in life, this is critically important. Seek out the people that are getting the best grades. Find out what they are doing. Is it how they study? Is it how they take notes? Are they using some special learning process? Talk to them, don't be afraid. Find out what they're doing and copy it. You do it too.

Apply a small 3FE analysis to the classroom itself in order to find out who these potential new-friends, tutors, teammates are:

Find out who they are

Focus on what they are doing

establish the **Fundamentals** of how they do what they do

Execute your imitating plan

Now, I didn't actually say *completing* all these tasks would be easy. No, in fact, becoming successful will be one of the hardest things you ever do. If your goal is to get in A in mathematics, just because you know how to do it, does not guarantee success. You may get a C out of the class. However, if you work hard, if you study, if you have a plan as to how to make the grade you desire, your C will be well earned. And, because you worked for it, and now know what you must do to achieve better results, the next math class may not be such a challenge. The next time, you may get the A.

2) LEARN HOW TO TAKE NOTES & READ TEXTBOOKS

I often tell people to consider how Reading Is Fundamental. Not only is RIF an organization but the organization's name is an unassailable fact. Education is the very foundation of any success, and if you are to leverage any tool effectively you must learn it, most especially when it is utilized in the furthering of your education. You must read, read, read, read, I say a thousand times read. As our culture changes far too many of us are limiting ourselves. We don't read for pleasure. We don't read to improve our mental capabilities. We just don't read. This must change.

You must commit to reading your textbook. You must commit to taking notes. You must commit to remaining engaged. The 3FE plan detailed above will lead you to working out ways of easing what may seem boring and tedious. Explore your options. There are methods for taking note. SEEK ANSWERS. Ask for help on note taking. Ask for help on a weekly plan to keep up with your reading. Ask for help on how to question yourself on the textbook material, so you can better master it. You can do all these things, if you only commit to doing so.

3) TUTORING SESSIONS

You may note that these classroom tools all seem to tie together. You must seek out others to help you be successful. You can copy what someone is doing in order to succeed in the classroom (and remember, this DOES NOT MEAN COPY THEIR WORK! NO CHEATING!) You seek the help of others in order to improve your ability to absorb the textbook material. You can seek help from others on helping you take better notes. You can, and must also seek out tutors, be they fellow students, or professionals. There's a wealth of services out there for all of us, anyone, and

I do mean anyone. Tutors can help you improve how you do your work, as well as help you actually understand the work on a deeper level. I even suggest tutors for those that are doing well, because additional information from others who have mastered the work can only improve your own chances at being an even greater success. Consider it critically.

4) TEACHERS & YOU

I don't think I really have to say much here. You may love your teacher. You may only like your teacher. You may dislike your teacher. You may hate your teacher. You may despise your teacher. But the fact of the matter is, that for a time a good portion of your year, you and that teacher are in it together. There are great teachers out there who will make it their business to stretch you, to push you, to goad you, to give you what you may not even want, a burning desire to win in the classroom. If this is your teacher, DO NOT JUST GO WITH THE FLOW!

You have an absolutely outstanding opportunity here. Don't waste it. Meet with this teacher. Get to know this teacher. Share your insights with this teacher. Drive, passion, and motivation are all inherently addictive, and they will make you enjoy the classroom all the more, and that can only make you a better student. However, we must also consider the converse. If your teacher is awful, if the two of you aren't getting along and not making it happen, then you, yes YOU have to take the reigns of responsibility and do something about it. I know this isn't fair. I know this isn't right. You expect, want, and need the best from your teachers. However, you must remember that your teachers are only human, they are fallible, just like the rest of us they are far from perfect beings. Some of their imperfections may spill out in the classroom. You must move past this and continue to work towards your success.

Partner with other students. Spend extra time on the material if you have a subpar teacher so that you can master it despite the teacher's failings. Seek the help of other teachers. Another teacher may even be teaching the same material. Just tell them you're looking to get ahead. And still try to connect to your teacher. Set aside time to talk to them, and see if there is anything you can do with them in order to improve the situation. At the very least, it's worth a try. And if nothing works, consider all your options. Do you need to transfer out of the classroom? Is the situation even more serious, requiring administrative involvement? Think critically about all your options, and never forget that you are there to get an education. That is your only goal.

5) PRIORITIZATION

Time management does not come easily to us humans, especially in our modern societies so filled with conveniences. Distractions plague us minute by minute, hour by hour. Our conveniences become inconveniences, especially when they sit in our hand or on our monitors and televisions. We lack focus. As Focus is core to 3FE it moves you to the frame of mind where you can start being consistent. In our multi-tasking society this will continue to be a challenge, but the tools will aid you in remaining focused on what's important. Part of this focus is making sure you've prioritized your tasks on a daily basis. I personally keep a To Do list that I go over every day. This simple task list is of immense utility. It's amazing that something so simple as a list can add such great benefit. Organization and prioritization are not to be taken for granted. Without them, you cannot be as effective, and a lack of effectiveness will prevent you from succeeding.

Below, is an example of a simple prioritized To Do list:

Priority	Task	Due Date
1	Read notes before Algebra Class	11/15 – this morning
2	Meet with Mr. Edwards on Chemistry assignment	11/15 @ 2:15
3	Beta Club Meeting	11/15 @ 2:45

4	Read History Assignment	11/15 – evening
5	Football Practice	11/15
6	Charity work with Coach	11/17
7	Work on English Term Paper	Daily – Due 12/8

6) HOW TO STUDY

Study hard. Study effectively. However, this does not mean you must study every single day with your back hunched over and head held low. No, the most important thing to consider when studying is how you study. First, commit to studying, but studying intelligently. Be smart about how you study. Put together your fundamental system for studying. Refer back to the prioritization list. If you prioritize your tasks, which include study time, and give them due dates, then you will know when to study. If you work hard at building your plan, and determine exactly how much effort you have to spend to make sure you cover all the material in a class, then you will know how long you have to study. And when you study, ask questions. Question yourself. Quiz your friends. Learn the material from every angle. Have several perspectives on the information you now possess. By doing this, you will achieve mastery over the material.

For more information on improving in the classroom reference my book: An Educational Primer for the Majority Student. I would also like to offer the three following books as references on HOW to study, and improve your performance. I also reference these books in my Primer. I personally think they're excellent and will serve to make you a much better student. Remember ... READ, READ, READ!!!

Three Study Books To Read

Getting Straight A's
by
Gordon Green

Getting Straight A's may be difficult for some of you. It can be used by students in high school, but it is geared more towards college students.

What Smart Students Know
by
Adam Robinson

Simply put, this book is fantastic. As I have said, I'm not an expert. However, in my opinion, Adam Robinson is.

Study Smarter not Harder
by
Kevin Paul

Kevin Paul has put together an easy to follow guide on academic improvement. He explains how each of us has the ability to become a genius.

Chapter 3

3FE For Who You Want To Be

My name is D.S. Brown, and I aspire to be the very best I can be. In particular, at this moment, I am indulging in a number of my personal passions, things that motivate me, that drive me forward in earnest, things that make me happy. What are they? I love to help people. I love to see people succeed. I love learning. I love expanding my horizons. I love reading. I most certainly love writing. So I am boldly aspiring to be, become, and grow in being … an author.

Wow, that just sounds so outstanding. I mean, I have to pat myself on the back. Makes me feel good, as it should. However, as stated in the last chapter I too must acknowledge my limits, even as I embrace my capabilities. There have been and there will be failures, outstanding failures, colossal failures due to my hubris, my stubbornness, my arrogance, my ignorance, and even my outright stupidity. Yep, my stone cold stupidity. I do stupid things too often to count. Ahhh well … still, I will never stop hoping, thinking, imagining.

As my father-in-law once said, "that one there … he's a dreamer."

I want you to dream. I want you to hope. I want you to aspire. In the doing, I offer a tool to help you distill your thoughts, separating fact from fantasy, focusing on what's real for you, as opposed to what will only surface in the recesses of your nightly dreams. We could work through this chapter focusing on how to leverage 3FE in order to become an author, or maybe a singer, dancer or actor. Maybe we could use this time and have you conduct a good, strong motivated analysis that points the way to fame and riches on the gridiron as a football star, or maybe a baseball player, or maybe you believe you can box, or drop the ball through the hoop as the next great basketball player. Maybe you're a soccer star. Maybe, maybe you're not thinking critically. In my books *Critical Success: The 2 Rules of 3*, and *An Educational Primer for the Majority Student*, I talk about why we must truly focus our attention away from these generalized aspirations and desires, these hopes and dreams that are cultivated by the insidious negative aspects of MDC, Media-Driven ConsumerCelebreality. We are not all meant to be superstar athletes and actors, or even minor athletes and actors, popular only in our own towns. It is critical that we embrace critical cognition and truly look at ourselves, look deeply in order to discern what we're truly passionate about, what we truly desire in our heart of hearts, and which of the things exist in great abundance at the crossroads of our passion and capability. What are we both good at and enjoy doing immensely?

Do you have a powerful sense of responsibility? Do you manage the stress of danger well, even as it erects challenges in your personal life? Do you have no fear of heights, no fear of imminent death due to unfortunate circumstance, do you see unrestrained, uncontrolled fire winding its deadly way through the environs of humanity's modern technology as something to be fought rigorously, abolished at the hands of dedicated men and women committed to ending the flame and saving the lives that stand in the line of the fire? Is this you? Does this make you happy? Do you have the physical, mental, and emotional spiritual strength to shoulder such a burden, the hours, the death, the lows, as well as the highs, and the gratitude from those that see you standing on the line, saving them from destruction? If this is you, then maybe you're meant to be in your heart of hearts, a fireman. Seek and know, and from there after identifying what you need in order to be a fireman, define the plan you need to execute in order to achieve your objective, and obtain Critical Success. And what is Critical Success?

Critical Success is the planned achievement of something urgent and essential, utilizing skillful planning and judgment for the express purpose of attaining personal prosperity.

However, as dramatic as this objective is, I would like to take two objectives and approach them as one, which will truly clear the way for you to pursue your higher objective of becoming exactly who it is you were born to be. First, within the confines of our modern society every single last one of us as citizens of this modern culture engaged in the consumer cycle of create, purchase, consume, and dispose must seek to BE this, must seek to achieve this as an objective, as a way of life.

Critical Success points the way towards satisfaction and opens the door to happiness. Truly it does. So, let's combine two into one and work through a 3FE exercise of determining who we want to be by first deciding and claiming the objective of being debt free, and thereby happy, which in the aggregate can truly unlock the gate to your own personal true pursuit of happiness.

So, our issue? We're saddled with debt. We're unhappy. What do we want to be? We want to be debt-free and happy. The tool for motivational empowerment rests firmly in our hand. We're ready to use it, to engage this problem, breaking it down, shattering it, and removing it as an obstacle in our life.

Let's lay out the scenario.

Benton Tucker looks happy. All his friends think he's happy. He has three beautiful children who attend private school. He lives in a $600,000 home on the edge of a lake in a pristine gated community. He drives an $80,000 luxury sedan. His wife drives a $65,000 luxury SUV. She's a stay at home mom. Every room in his home is furnished. They take great vacations. He has a golf club membership. One of his wife's all-time favorite hobbies is shopping. Benton's salary? He makes about $198,000 a year. He has credit card debt that might boggle the minds of lesser men … or so he believes them to be lesser men. However, he has a very, very hard time sleeping. He sweats a lot, even when it's cold. Sometimes he convulses, and he doesn't know why. He does note it seems to happen whenever he hears the word *buy*. He tells people he's happy. However, he has noticed that his face hurts a lot. He smiles all the time, but the corners of his mouth hurt, like his smile was pasted on his face with super glue.

I have debt, but it's fine. I'm really very happy!

Please consider this critically my friends. Really happy people don't go around telling people how happy they are. They just are. Such a statement is very telling. It reveals much about Benton's state of mind, and can very well tell us a great deal about the state of his body. Stress is powerfully debilitative. In fact, it can kill. Some of you may remember that commercial Lending Tree used to have on television where the guy had a perpetual smile on his face. He revealed that he was in debt up to his eyeballs, and then reached out and implored, begged for somebody to help him.

This is the state of many of us today who have fallen victim to MDC (Media-Driven ConsumerCelebreality) and the worship of status and material possessions. Our culture has driven us to literally take leave of our senses, and imbibe at the fount of financial despair. And the bad thing about it is the drink that comes out of that fount tastes great, like Kool-Aid for you non-drinkers, or a fine expensive scotch or cognac for those of you that partake. Of course, the problem is the drink has a wicked awful aftertaste that you can readily become accustomed to, and it completely rots your insides all to bits. This … is us stuck in debt. This, is Benton Tucker, on the edge of a heart attack, on the edge of death.

Grab hold people. Let's embrace 3FE and get motivated. Let's get empowered. Let us get hold of a proper mindset, maintain a positive attitude, and be prepared to make the hard decisions for ourselves and our posterity. Let's proceed to conduct a quick and succinct, but highly effective 3FE analysis on Benton's situation and solve this most vexing and vital issue. Let's figure out who he wants to be and what he needs to do. Let's make Benton debt-free and happy. First, let's review the model for the basics.

3FE	Find ... Focus ... establish the Fundamentals ... Execute!!! **Issue:**
Find	Identify the issue. Find what it is. Open your eyes, ready your mind, set your attitude to full on positive and engage in true critical thinking. Question everything, and then write it down. Who ... What ...Where ...When ... Why... How
Focus	Look closely at what you've found. Focus on it. These pieces of information aren't truly information yet. It's all just data. Dig into the details and clarify the bits and pieces of the data. Take note of the relationships between the bits of data. What additional details are there to consider?
Fundamentals	As the relationships between the data points becomes clear, a path arises from the data, and things begin to make sense. When data has meaning, it becomes information. Information has value and inherently can lend itself to a solution. This is the **F**undamentals, the essential tasks that bind the information together into action steps to resolve the issue.
Execute	Because sometimes you need an execution plan. Maybe you're going to execute in phases. Maybe you'll execute in one fell swoop, all at once. However, you do it, do it with emphasis! EXECUTE! EXECUTE! EXECUTE!

Now, we've covered the framework once again. Let's proceed in earnest. We'll act as though we're Benton, and conduct his analysis for him.

3FE	Find ... Focus ... establish the Fundamentals ... Execute!!! **ISSUE 1: Getting Debt-Free & Happy**
Find	**Who:** Me, Benton Tucker. I'm struggling. I think I'm about to go insane. I'm not happy at all, and I know why. I'm going to die. **What:** I've got a ton of debt. I can't afford my house. I can't afford my cars. I can't afford this lifestyle. I'm going to die. **Where**: Here, there, everywhere. I'm not happy wherever I go because the thought of everything falling down around me follows me wherever I go. However, in particular I guess the where is in my home. The issues seem to be in my home. **When:** It's constant, but it hits hardest every two weeks ... payday. **Why:** I'll be honest with myself. It happened so fast. There was so much out there. I make good money. I wanted so much. My wife wanted so much, and still wants it. It just happened so fast. **How:** Flowing cash and credit cards. No one told me no. There's time. It just seemed like I could manage to make it all fit. The cards and the cash, and a lack of the truth I guess. Yes, that's how. There is no truth.

Focus	**My Cars, My House, My Cards:** The cars are just too expensive. I pay around $2000 a month on car notes alone ... and one is a lease. I just can't keep up with 'em. My mortgage is just plain ridiculous. I have to pay $3500 a month. I'm making minimum payments on ten different credit cards. All but one is maxed out. I'm just drowning in debt, and my wife goes shopping every weekend. EVERY SINGLE WEEKEND! This is my breakdown: 1. Mortgage is my death. 2. Car Notes are my death. 3. Credit Card Bills are my death. 4. Lack of extra cash is my death. My golf clubs are the only things that seem to keep my sane. I lose myself when I play golf. But it's expensive too. I have to be honest. Everything in my life is leading to my death. I think I just might be ready to die. **Solution:** I have a spending problem. I have a priority problem. I have a management problem. I want to do the right thing and pay my debts. I just can't. And I can't seem to stop the bleeding of money from my pockets. Okay, okay, the truth, I can. It's just really, really hard. In the book Critical Success: The 2 Rules of 3 there is a 10 Point Plan for achieving Critical Success. I am going to follow it. In each area of my problem, there is a solution, a painful solution, but a solution that can work.

1. I need to try to refinance my house. This probably won't work. I'll have to break this down into levels. Either I funnel more of my monthly budget or we have to move. First, we'll see if we can't budget it. We're not behind yet. If we fall behind, then we start looking to move. Better yet, I'll look for options ahead of time just in case. If I can't negotiate a good deal with the bank, then we walk away from the house. It has to be an option.

2. I'm getting rid of the cars. That's the bottom line. We can't afford them. We don't need them. I'm replacing the cars with used cars that we can afford.

3. I'm calling a Credit Counseling Service. I'm cutting up all my cards but one. The one I keep I'm putting in the freezer. Only for emergencies.

4. The kids will have to go to public school. The schools around here are pretty darn good anyway.

5. And ... I'm quitting the golf club.

6. My wife will have to get a job. She has three degrees. It may be hard to find a position, but she's going to have to try. We need the income.

7. My wife is going to go crazy. Just to make sure we make it through I'm putting aside some money to go see a marriage counselor. Our marriage needs a tune-up and I refuse to let money break us apart.

	Cash Flow: I get paid every two weeks. We're going to have to build a budget and stick to it. We'll check the budget every Sunday evening. We'll document all our receipts. We'll make sure we're covering our necessities. For the time-being, there will be no wants. No extras. We're going to have to go really lean. **Solution:** I know I'm supposed to pay myself first and then pay everybody else. But I'll be honest. I'll feel better once I get some of this debt knocked out. I'll go lean for three months. Then, I'll start paying myself first. I'll follow 3POP after about two years of going lean, and put 3POP in the budget. I will embrace the Three Principles of Prosperity. - Invest some of my cash in the Capital Markets. - Work towards land ownership, after I have a grip on the land I currently own. - I do have an idea for a business. I'll set aside some cash for an entrepreneurial dream I've had for some time. **I NEED TO BE HAPPY!!!!!** All the above is a down payment on my happiness. It can work. It has to work. I have to believe it will work. If it doesn't, I'm just gonna die. **Solution:** I'm gonna read that poem Attitude by Charles Swindoll every morning before work. If I change my attitude and do all the other things ... maybe I won't die.
Fundamentals	**Task 1: Sit the family down!** Explain to everyone just how much trouble we're in, and how serious it is. Then, tell them we have a plan, but it's going to require a lot of sacrifice.

	Task 2: Put together my two-tiered mortgage plan. I'll try to keep up with the mortgage. I'll try to refinance. If that doesn't work, we're moving, the house can go to you know where, along with the furniture and everything else in it!!!!
	Task 3: SELL THE CARS! I'll try to cover the outstanding balance, but that's not likely. I'll do what I can. I'll buy two used old cars cash. I can do that with two months worth of checks. I just need to balance it right. If not, then I'll buy just one used car. BUT I DON'T WANT THE LUXURY CARS ANYMORE!!! They're giving me gas!
	Task 4: Schedule a meeting with a Credit Counseling Service.
	Task 5: Cut all my credit cards accept one.
	Task 6: Put the remaining card in a cup of water and freeze it. It'll be to thaw only in emergencies.
	Task 7: Put the kids in Public School.
	Task 8: Quit the golf club.
	Task 9: Find a marriage counselor/therapist and schedule an appointment.
	Task 10: Wife looks for job.
	Task 11: Put together new budget and review it every Sunday.
	Task 12: Put together tactical plan for lean 3 to 6 months.
	Task 13: Put together strategic plan for savings and 5 year plan that includes 3POP.
	Task 14: Stay positive. Read the poem Attitude.
Execute	I can't wait another minute. I'm executing my plan starting RIGHT NOW!

It looks like Mr. Benton Tucker is well on his way to being happy ... if he can manage to stick to the plan he's laid out. It's ambitious, challenging, and a stark reality for far too many people in today's modern materialistic society. Benton was clearly on the edge. He's terribly upset. As many of us know, stress can kill. He's already predicting his death ... he even seems to long for it. However, he isn't longing for it that bad. Though he's in deep pain he had the strength necessary to push forward, to desire a way out, to want happiness and actually seek it.

Benton Tucker achieved a milestone in life. He became what he wanted to be, which is what some call a salary-man, a white collar job. He has a career in a field that affords him a high paying salary. However, once he attained that objective he rapidly lost sight and could no longer be what he wanted to be, which was simply happy. He thought material trappings would add to his happiness. In fact, it only brought him pain and ever closer to ruin. He most certainly has a very long way to go; however, by using the tool he's now able to chart a course back towards happiness. He'll be able to remove his problems and focus on being the man he wants to be.

Now, you can use the tool to determine which course you want to take in life. You can use it to actually define which career path you want to take. You can use it to determine what job you think might be most rewarding, where you might be happiest. You can use it to chart a change in your career path, to make a life decision that allows you to achieve balance between responsibility and passion, what you need to do to survive and take care of your own, and at the same time fuel your desire to do something that you truly enjoy. Or, you can use it to throw caution to the wind and fully embrace what makes you happiest, even if it doesn't make you a lot of money.

You have to find a personal mandate. You must make it an absolute MUST. You have to chart a course through life that allows you to be the best you, you can be. Who you are is within you. You simply need to discover exactly who you are. Use 3FE as a light to show you the way.

Deep within all of us there is a beacon. It may be out, no heat no light. It may be dim, a small thing with only a sliver of hope to burn bright. Its state really is of no consequence. The point is it's there. It's inside. And it's waiting. It has been there since your conception. It is the nova of your potential. A veritable star at the heart of your spirit, waiting to be fed the fuel it needs in order to grow, and burn bright. By determining who you are, by discovering your passion, you gain perspective, you understand your truth, you feed the light. Work on that which is closest to the true you, and that light will grow, and grow, and burn, and become unto a celestial beacon, a nova of spirit that not only brightly lights the path forward for you, but through you words, actions, and positivity serves as a beacon, a guidepost for others.

Chapter 4

IDENTIFYING 3FE IN PEOPLE

Who are the people? When they come together how do we see them? How can we see them? Or rather, how can we leverage 3FE to see them from a perspective that is team oriented, complimentary to what they bring to the table, and highly effective?

We are going to take a break from solving actual problems and instead now focus on the constituent parts of the tool for motivational empowerment and examine how we can leverage the tool as a team paradigm, a metaphor for actual people, and how they can be representative of the tool itself and come together with their particular assets to solve problems and resolve real-world issues.

We have an issue before us as. We have something that must be addressed. You are going to be held accountable. You are responsible. Even if someone else isn't holding you accountable, you've embraced a higher level or responsibility. You're an aspiring critical thinker and you truly do provide due consideration in any given situation. You question effectively and dive deep. You think logically and rationally. You don't forget the human component and operate with empathy and compassion where the human component is concerned. And within our critical summation the human component is what we are discussing.

Who are the Finders on the team? Who are the Focusers? Who are the Fundamental planners? And finally, who are the Executers. We use different words to describe people and how they interact with one another. We use different words to describe the contributions they may make to any effort we undertake. In terms of the tool for motivational empowerment let's consider a positive categorization of people for different aspects of the tool, leveraging what they do best in order to create a wholly more effective team. You, as the implementer of 3FE on your team can help guide the group in this endeavor, and thereby break out assigned tasks accordingly in order to achieve optimal results. It's even better when your team has gelled and they naturally tend to do this on their own.

Let's use a specific scenario in order to work our way through a 3FE exercise assigning people to roles within our inspirational methodology. We'll review this scenario later as an analysis exercise. For your consideration we have an emergency issue in the workplace that requires the efforts of a focus team. This team is charged with resolving the problem in a rapid-fire fashion. In this example we'll be making use of a five person 3FE unit. The team will consist of Margaret Sutton, Andy Cho, Talia Coleridge, Larry Jackson, and Ronald Bread.

Margaret Sutton has found herself over the last year. She has blossomed as a senior project manager in her organization and is being considered for rapid promotion into management. She comes from a technical background in software development but found her gifts in managing people and tasks. Her ability to meld people and tasks together in a strong plan has been of great benefit. She has utilized her technical skills to dive deep into the details and understand the developer's tasks without interfering. She's used her people skills to effectively motivate her project teams. All of these skills together have become absolutely essential to her success. She recently became acquainted with 3FE and has learned how to utilize it within the Systems Development Life Cycle for projects. It has made her more effective in total and has allowed her to execute her solutions at varying speeds for maximum effect. It's all in the planning.

Andy Cho is what we call hard core. He is a developer's developer, the programmer's programmer, cut from the old cloth in terms of knowing his tasks, enjoying his tasks, avoiding needless interaction with other people and staying deep in his tasks. That is what he likes to do. That is all he really wants to do. He likes solving tough problems. He thoroughly enjoys the complexities of coding. Software development is his dream, and fresh out of college he's experiencing it. He's not like some of his fellow developers, multitaskers that enjoy layers of social interaction through their gadgets, or even glad-handling management because they either actually enjoy it or can better tolerate it. Andy doesn't even care to see his management. In his mind, management appearing equals problems. These are issues he will have to address over the course of his career, but for now, this is where he is in life.

Talia Coleridge is a specialist in the systems field. She has received several accolades over the course of her career. Her skills as a programmer are still as sharp as they ever were. However, her knowledge and capabilities have grown, become more expansive. She's able to program in a host of computer languages. She's familiar with a host of development tools. She's a qualified database expert and systems architect. She is what we call, a guru.

Larry Jackson is a friend of Andy's. They went to the same school. He has a technical background as well but is very much wedded to project management. He loves shepherding projects to completion with no defects. He has managed several small projects since joining the company and has been trusted with medium sized projects as the sole project manager responsible for delivery. Margaret has taken it upon herself to mentor him in his career and brought him onboard her latest project as the project manager for batch processing and core data integration. So far, his performance has been exemplary. But, things don't always work out as planned.

Ronald Bread is the project's DevOps Manager in charge of the development pipeline. He is responsible for environment control, migration, and application integration and stability. He oversees the whole product pipline and makes sure it moves from the development environment to the production environment with quality built-in and operating as advertised.

The team has just celebrated the release of their new integrated intelligent ordering system. There is a batch process that runs every night to update pricing information, logistical data, and pending orders. All data is sourced and linked through a repository of data marts that pulls just-in-time data assortments from a core enterprise data warehouse. New orders are requested through new versatile and dynamic web-based customer apps that live in the company's secure cloud. Orders are generated, inventories are updated, and orders are transmitted to the vendors for processing and fulfillment. The entire project has gone through one full week of processing, and so far things have been running perfectly. This effort is the company's crowning jewel; its master achievement capping two years of incremental development. Now, it's early Thursday morning, and processing has just run into the proverbial brick wall, and all HECK is breaking loose.

"I think we have a problem," muttered Andy. He was watching system jobs process on his screen. The jobs ran several computer programs updating various databases and producing records for transmission. One job turned red, then another, and another, then three more at the same time. The rest of the processing stream ground to a dead halt. Margaret was at the front of the room monitoring progress from her own screen. Everything turned bright red. She looked up.

"Andy?" She asked. "What's the deal?"

Her voice was steady, in control, but tinged with a sense of heightened concern. They were only a couple of hours from the start of the business day. There was no time left for mistakes. It was do or die.

"I don't know," he said, as his fingers moved rapidly across the keyboard. "Several jobs are going down at once. Looks like there's some kind of problem with the controller too. I can't dig into the job to see what the problem is."

Almost immediately the phones started ringing. A representative was in the control room for each area of the company. This effort touched all departments, and no part of the company lacked representation. Support developers sitting at their desks, and some at home in the wee hours of the morning had been monitoring progress on their own screens. They saw the failure and recognized the impact. This could bring the entire company to its knees.

However, the model for the control room was one of consummate efficiency. The executive who set this effort in motion was actually not on duty, but her leadership throughout had been outstanding. She had set the tone for the entire project, and she had placed her trust in Margaret. Margaret furrowed her eyebrows, every bit the leader. She would not let her down, not her executive, not her team, not her company. In her mind a fire started, a critical thinking fire. She went into action.

"Ronald?"

"I'm already on it," he said. "Gimme a second."

"You only got a second. Time's of the essence."

He frowned, just a bit. He didn't need her to tell him that. The butterflies in his stomach told him that.

Andy glanced back at him from his screen. "I can't see nuthin'.'

"I know Andy. Hang on. Just gimme a sec."

"I'll take a look," Talia said, offering her expertise. "Logging into the scheduler now."

"Just gimme a sec," Ronald say, more testily. He didn't want anyone doing his job for him.

"Talia and Ronald, both of you stay on it," Margaret said, just as the phone on her desk started ringing. She knew exactly who it was. "Larry, you're on standby."

"Got it," Larry said. He knew what his role would be. Right now, his job was to keep a close eye on the team, but stay out of the way and let them work.

"All of you guys are my SWAT team," Margaret said. "Wake it up and stay frosty. Now, lemme take this call."

They all risked a quick glance up, looking at her. She stood at her desk as she took the call. They knew exactly who it was and wondered how much heat they would be able to feel through the phone.

"Yes," Margaret said to the executive on the other end of the line. "Yes. Yes, absolutely. I was just getting ready to send out a communication. No. No, we don't. Impact would be severe, but I'm certain we can get a hold of it. No, not by the start of business. We'll have an outage. I've got my team together and I'll give you an update every 30 minutes until this thing is resolved. Yes. Thank you."

She hung up the phone. "Let's get on it, people."

The team's glancing had turned into a surreptitious stare. They wanted to know what the word was, and if it would burn. Apparently, the conversation had not been that bad at all. However, if they didn't get the situation straightened out, the next phone call was likely to not be so nice. No, not so nice at all.

"This is a comedy of errors," Ronald said. "We've got a corruption."

"I see it," Talia said. "Across the server farm. We've got other jobs that may be impacted. Other applications that may start to break down."

"Can we contain it?" Margaret asked.

Ronald answered before Talia could beat him to it. "It's already contained. I installed the scheduler's modular systems fail-safes. It was considered optional. I thought it was mandatory."

Talia smiled. "Good call, Ronald."

"We've got ten boxes effected," he said. "They're the ordering and ordering reporting systems. Sales and Credit are still online and running. They'll complete on time and meet their SLA's."

SLA is short for Service Level Agreement. An agreed upon time between the Information Tech teams and the business customer as to when systems would be online and available for use.

"Great," said Margaret. "At least we have that saving grace.

No upper level executives hazing us about sales reports."

"Keep 'em happy," said Talia.

Margaret smiled. "All part of the job. So, what's our status on the rest, Ronald?"

"Half and half, I think. Andy, I've made a configuration change. You should be able to see your jobs results. I can't restart them though."

Andy had been clicking away at his machine for the last few minutes while they were conversing, his face buried deep into his screen. Larry had come over to join him. Neither one of them looked happy.

"Did you hear me, Andy?" Ronald asked.

"He heard you," Larry said. "Kinda focused on something."

"Larry?" Margaret asked. "Andy, one of you speak up."

Larry sighed. "Looks like we've got a bigger problem. The data itself is corrupted. We've got several bad files."

"How bad?"

"Don't know. Andy's digging."

Margaret looked at Talia. "I'm already on it," Talia said, as her fingers quickly flew across her keyboard. "Let's examine a few data dumps and see what it looks like."

"I can already tell you," Andy said. "We'll have to rebuild all our driving files. The corruption is across the board."

"Rerun all of the ordering batch!?!" Margaret asked, her voice rising.

"We'll lose some time," Talia said. "We won't make our SLA, but we knew that already. The good thing is the new data system is architected for multiple redundancies at critical checkpoints. It's not the old day's Margaret."

Margaret smiled at her Systems Specialist. Talia had worked on architecting the system herself. She knew it backwards and forwards. She was the pre-eminent failsafe.

"I've already isolated our restart points on batch. Andy, check your board."

"Got it," he said. "But I can't do anything about it."

"I'm working on it!" Ronald said, with a bit more volume in his voice than was probably necessary. He was clearly getting frustrated.

They had system redundancy, which means they didn't lose everything. They could recover from the corruption. They still had some issues on the scheduler, which would take time to correct. Was there anything else?

Margaret pulled out a piece of paper and drew a large standing rectangle. She broke the rectangle into four sections, and labeled them: Find, Focus, establish the Fundamentals, and Execute. She wrote a name next to each word in its section. In her mind she saw her team, their roles, and how she would quickly navigate this problem to resolution. She'd faced this kind of pressure before. It was wearying in its repetition, energy consuming, but readily doable. She was motivated, and in her mind she was already halfway to the finish line. She wrote down the details of what they already knew in the Find box.

"Do we know what caused the corruption? If we restart, how do we know we won't encounter it again?"

Quiet.

"I think Andy's onto something," Larry said. "He's looking into it."

Margaret considered the situation. A status call would be starting soon. She owed the world a status update. She had facts. She needed more facts. She looked up and saw Talia standing with Ronald. The team was in action. She composed an email and sent it to the entire organization. The team was doing what the team needed to do. She trusted them, and knew she needed to take a back seat for a while. They were in what she liked to call the fifteen & thirty phase. She needed an update every fifteen minutes to keep herself from going batty. She had to update the world every thirty minutes to keep all the executives from going batty and dropping a hammer on her head.

No worries. She was a superior communicator.

Fifteen minutes later, even as she was holding onto her

patience, she glanced at Larry and Andy, and saw both of them smiling. Talia drifted over to stand with them. She started smiling too, pointing at the screen and making some direct suggestions, things apparently they should pay particular attention to. This … was a very good sign. But of course, very good was always relative. She wanted to ask what was going on immediately. She waited for a count of thirty, and was pleasantly rewarded.

"We've got it," Larry said. "Looks like a couple of programs had some bugs in them. They were creating the bad data. Also, it looks like they were passing parameters to the scheduler that were junk, messing up system memory, which caused the failure on the scheduler."

"We'll have to reboot the servers," Ronald chimed in. "I can do that pretty fast, then I'll have to re-load the scheduler, and set it to start executing from the break point before the corruption set in, using our backed up data of course. I'll need to double-check everything, and then I should be good to go."

"That is outstanding," Margaret said.

"Let me put together a quick action plan," Larry interrupted. "We want to make sure we're all clear on what we have to do. Andy has to make his code changes really, really fast. And test them."

"Once they're ready I'll make sure they get moved to the override library for execution," Talia said. "We'll double check the program changes later for permanent production install."

"Yep," Larry nodded. "So give me a few minutes and I'll have our plan laid out. We can review it, and if we're all good. We'll execute."

Margaret smiled. Larry was her guy. "Get to it," she said.

During the lull Margaret added to her list of information in the Find box. She also went ahead and elaborated on those statements in the Focus box, along with statements that clarified what would be required to resolve the overall issue. She wrote a bit more, amended her notes, and then moved to the next box. Instead of writing, she put her pen down. She looked up at her team, letting her eyes settle on Larry.

A few more minutes passed as Larry feverishly worked his laptop, calling to various team members, getting their input, identifying their tasks in priority order. This was a quick, fast, down and dirty action plan. There were no listings of task durations, low-level descriptions of sub-tasks, and complicated dependencies. This was aggressive execution, taking the best of a project manager's skills, leveraging strong communication, and trust among the team members, understanding that they knew how to do their jobs, even as he asked those necessary critical questions that could help each person illuminate any missed details regarding what they have to do, and better help the whole team achieve success. It didn't take him long. He was a man on the move, growing and getting better and better.

"Here's what we've got," he said, requesting Margaret's attention. The rest of the team looked at Larry as he read from his laptop.

"We'll be operating on two core tasks at the same time. Andy has three programs that he's modified. He's moved them to staging and Talia will move them to the override library for execution. He'll work with Talia to make sure the right files are available from the backups for processing. Ronald will monitor movement of the programs and files to the production environment and ensure everything is ready. He's the third eye we need to ensure efficacy. Ronald will restart the scheduling servers and the app, double check the right input files are available, make the appropriate adjustments to the schedule, and then hit the red button. And from there we'll be processing for maybe the next couple of hours, if that. Ronald thinks he can tune-up the processing power on the servers as the jobs are running in the highest priority. He thinks he might be able to gain anywhere from a twenty to forty percent increase in performance."

That was something new.

"Can you really, Ronald?" Margaret asked.

Ronald nodded rather confidently. "Yes ma'am. I'm certain I can crank out at least 20 percent, if not more."

"Excellent!"

"And that's it," Larry said. "From there, we monitor, and keep our fingers crossed."

"Sounds good," Margaret said. "Any callouts? Any questions?"

Everyone was silent.

"Taking it down the line," she added, being more direct.

"Talia?" She asked. Talia shook her head. "Plan is sound. I'm in full agreement."

"Ronald?"

"Let's do it," he said.

"Andy?"

Andy's head was down, close to his screen, all his focus on the machine, none on the world around him.

"Andy?" Margaret repeated. Larry reached back and hit him on the head.

"Yes!" Andy said, snapping up straight. "I'm good."

"No thoughts, concerns about the plan?"

"None. Let's do it already."

Everybody chuckled. "Larry?" Margaret asked.

Larry looked around at the team, took a deep breath, and shook his head. "I think this is it. Let's pull the trigger."

Her team had spoken. That was all she needed. "Larry, send me the plan so I can compose the enterprise status message. The call will be starting soon. I'll let you speak to the plan."

Larry smiled, sensing an opportunity. "Yes, ma'am."

"Alright everybody … EXECUTE!"

Margaret had developed her SWAT team over time. They were each very skilled at their jobs, and they avoided needless negative conflict by leveraging each other's gifts and contributing within their various roles. Some of them had the knowledge and skill to traverse multiple roles, and contribute in different areas. However, at their core, given the way their team was constructed, they each played a pivotal part, and could be categorized in terms of the 3FE model. This actually helped Margaret in clarifying her team's strengths and effectiveness. She could help guide them to peak proficiency and didn't need to micro-manage them at all. They had all bonded and established trust, and as the leader, she fully understood them and could when needed aggressively engage them in a positive manner, giving them the appropriate room to excel, solve, and add value. The methodology helped her understand this, the model clarified this. 3FE was her tool to propel them all forward.

    Can you guess which person played which role? Below I've provided Margaret's 3FE exercise for this emergency situation. In it she identifies who was responsible for what area, adding value to the entire effort in their individual roles. Once again, I show the base model and its outline with instructional information at each stage of the methodology. Margaret's actual example follows.

3FE	Find ... Focus ... establish the Fundamentals ... Execute!!! **Issue:**
Find	Identify the issue. Find what it is. Open your eyes, ready your mind, set your attitude to full on positive and engage in true critical thinking. Question everything, and then write it down. Who ... What ...Where ...When ... Why ... How!
Focus	Look closely at what you've found. Focus on it. These pieces of information aren't truly information yet. It's all just data. Dig into the details and clarify the bits and pieces of the data. Take note of the relationships between the bits of data. What additional details are there to consider?
Fundamentals	As the relationships between the data points becomes clear, a path arises from the data, and things begin to make sense. When data has meaning, it becomes information. Information has value, and inherently can lend itself to a solution. These are the Fundamentals, the essential tasks that bind the information together into action steps that resolve the issue.
Execute	Because sometimes you need an execution plan. Maybe you're going to execute in phases. Maybe you'll execute in one fell swoop, all at once. However, you do it, do it with emphasis! EXECUTE! EXECUTE! EXECUTE!

Margaret's 3FE team and problem solving analysis:

3FE	Find ... Focus ... establish the Fundamentals ... Execute!!! **ISSUE 1: Solving An Emergency Information Technology System Problem**
Find **Andy Cho**	**Who:** My team is trying to complete processing to have our applications available for the company. **What:** We're not going to meet our SLA (Service Level Agreement) because batch processing is halted. **Where**: We have a problem on the servers responsible for running our batch processes. **When:** We're in the early hours of the morning with little time left. **Why:** The jobs stopped running because of one, possibly many processing errors. We have to dig deeper to understand why. **How:** Unknown, under analysis. Andy is my main programmer on duty. I need him to do some detective work and figure this mess out.
Focus: **Talia Coleridge**	**Order Batch Processing:** Thirty Batch Jobs are down and applications will not be available. Closer examination determined that the outage was limited to the ordering and order reporting systems. Other vital core processing systems like sales and credit were not impacted. *We can still run a cash register and take a credit card ... whew!*

Solution: Ronald had installed an optional systems failsafe that prevented the failure from spreading. He'll have to get an accommodation for forward thinking. The solution is to restart batch. I'll have Talia aide the team on focusing on the how.

Ten specific servers are failing: The servers that process those jobs are causing errors.

Solution: Triage the boxes and isolate the error. Clearly the boxes will have to be rebooted. The team will have to save the logs if they can't isolate the problem quickly enough. The main goal for now is to get the boxes functioning again.

We can't diagnose the problem with the batch jobs: The error in the scheduler is preventing us from seeing how the job failed. This is a very strange error that we haven't seen before.

Solution: Isolate the error in the scheduler and get it running again so we can view the jobs and determine how they failed, what has to be changed, and how we can get them restarted.

Schedule Controller is failing: In all likelihood tied to whatever error is preventing us from seeing how the jobs failed.

Solution: Diagnose the problem and restart the scheduler. Ronald really needs to focus on this, with Talia backing him up.

Data Files are corrupted: The data files that the jobs are processing are useless. They've been corrupted.

	Solution: Intelligent Data Redundancy systems are in place and we have specific files on backup that we can use in each job, picking up processing directly from where we left out. Talia's architecture on this was absolutely exemplary. **We have bugs in main programs:** Looks like there were three programs that had bugs in them. The team considers the bugs minor but their impact was major. *In computer systems, sometimes that's just how it goes.* **Solution:** Andy with Talia advising is going to quickly make program changes, test them and then run them in place of the bad programs we have in production.
Fundamentals: **Larry Jackson**	**Task 1:** Andy modifies and tests bug fixes to three programs. **Task 2:** Andy moves his programs to staging. **Task 3:** Talia moves them to the override library to run in production. **Task 4:** Talia and Andy ensure the right files from the redundancy system are available and ready for execution. **Task 5:** Ronald will monitor all this activity. **Task 6:** Ronald will reboot the servers. **Task 7:** Ronald will double and triple check that we have the right programs and files available. **Task 8:** Ronald will make the appropriate adjustments to the schedule to ensure we restart at the point of failure. **Task 9:** Ronald will restart batch.

	Task 10: Ronald will fine-tune the schedule in progress to ensure it runs at the highest priority, which means in the least amount of time.
Execute **Ronald Bread**	Ronald is the executer. Once the plan has been validated, he will be the main person executing it, with support from the team, and oversight from Margaret and Larry.

Chapter 5
3FE On The Job

In the previous chapter we discussed applying 3FE and identifying how people can take on certain roles within the methodology, executing tasks that describe each phase of 3FE, perhaps playing to their strengths, those skills that make them most effective. We used a real-world example in the workplace in order to illustrate this concept.

In this chapter we're going to discuss how each individual on a given team can utilize 3FE to further their own objectives on the job. Consider, you're on a team and based on the information we discovered about people executing effectively on teams you realized you were a **Focuser**. Well, even though you may be a **Focuser** on a given team, you can still utilize all four phases of 3FE in order to pursue your personal objectives on the job.

Are you looking to get a promotion?

Or, is it that you're trying to make yourself simply a better worker, elevate your current standing in your position. Are you trying to become the best in your position? Or, is it something more dire? Are you at the end of your rope so to speak, and you're afraid they're about to fire you? You can't get along with your boss and you just have the hardest time meeting his or her expectations? You don't know quite what to do? Do you see others being successful, but you just can't make it happen for yourself? Do you need help? You can reach for the tool for motivational empowerment and help yourself.

I'll tell you the truth. I find myself utilizing 3FE every single day at work. I exercise it on an almost subconscious level. It creeps into my lexicon when I'm in discussions. It has been of inestimable value in helping me be a more effective manager. When I first developed the tool I vetted it, so to speak, in my own work environment. I'll be honest, it worked without fail, but sometimes forces in the workplace are beyond your control, and either you, or your boss, or you both together need a change. That's what happened to me. I utilized 3FE and met all my manager's expectations … until we arrived at a point where our worlds no longer coincided, and it was best for us to part ways. That's also a strong part of 3FE, and it was the effective utilization of the tool that led me to that conclusion, which I relayed in a personal discussion. We agreed, and everything turned out for the best.

Allow me to illustrate 3FE in the workplace by guiding you through two examples, the first is my own personal experience, the second the experience of someone else. I'll show you how 3FE became absolutely essential during this pivotal time in my life. How did it start?

Let me be frank. My boss was literally driving me insane. In retrospect I realized we had simply grown apart in terms of how we viewed my position and my responsibilities. I have to consider myself incredibly lucky, which is simply preparation and opportunity right? I was prepared for the change that needed to be made as I came to this crossroads in my life. I had proven myself time and time again, which afforded me the opportunity to work elsewhere in the organization, after we agreed that was the right course of action for me. I was able to make this change on the cusp of my boss taking some specific actions that might have adversely affected my career. A little bit of luck and a whole lot of preparedness saved the day. However, most people in the workforce don't get this choice. They don't have that option. It is, as they say, do or die. That makes the decision you have to make incredibly more difficult. Sometimes, you have no choice but to consider cutting your loses, and deciding for yourself how you'll end your tenure, before someone ends it for you. Will you resign? Or, will you allow yourself to get fired? The decision may require a very careful 3FE analysis. When faced with such a situation you must weigh your options thoroughly and then decide.

In my particular situation, I was being driven, in my humble opinion, to the proverbial brink of insanity. My father-in-law was deathly ill from cancer, to which he would succumb in a year. My wife was five months pregnant. And my boss thought I was quickly becoming worthless. We were simply at loggerheads, and it was awful.Things weren't happening for me. I was losing focus. I was getting confused. I no longer had a plan I could execute. I was flailing and failing.

Interestingly enough I have since grown into accepting the truth. The failure was twofold and must be owned by us both. I could not manage to meet and maintain what my manager perceived to be the appropriate expectation level. I would perceive success. My manager would perceive failure. And even when my manager acknowledged some level of low-grade success my manager would swiftly in the moment point out were my success was really and truly quite piss-poor and that there were at the very least ten to fifteen different things I could have done far better.

Objectives were still achieved. The team thought I was going great at my primary job, serving as an effective buffer, taking the brunt of her criticisms, and sheltering them from the fallout. They often said the day was far better when they did not have to see her. And there I was, still defending her, telling them to please see her differently, even while my manager cheerfully kicked me up one side and kicked me down the other. You see, I really did care for my boss. I thought highly of her then, and I think highly of her still. I would not be who I am if not for her.

Still, sometimes in our roles as workers we don't see ourselves, or the effects of our approach. Sometimes, we simply no longer see each other at all. Fighting through this, even when I did meet her lowered expectations, wasn't doing my career any good at all. My manager talked to her peers and upper management. The perception of my being a failure became a creeping thing, infecting the rest of the management team, building filters over eyes that at once saw me as a rising star, now a slowly petering flame, destined to burn out. I would have to deal with this perception for several more years.

I could not, I would not accept this.

My recently developed 3FE methodology became my essential tool for my own motivational success. And of course, at this point I had absolutely nothing to lose. I felt as though I was on a ledge. I could feel the world swaying beneath my feet every single day I walked into the building. With each passing hour it felt as though my manager was getting closer and closer to her freeing and breath saving goal, and my eventual downfall. I could feel my termination right around the corner. I was going to be fired.

Now, this might not have been true, but I know many of you out there have felt this way, seen what looked like very clear writing on the wall. And as is most normal you became quite desperate for a way out. Yes, I was getting desperate, but not for a way out under my own terms. No, I didn't want out. I decided what I needed was another way in. I refused to be shown the door. There was another path, and in my mind it meant meeting her where we needed to meet, to deal with what to me appeared to be functioning insanity, for as long as necessary, until that internal door opened and I could readily walk through it to a better opportunity.

Incidentally, that's exactly what happened, to my sheer and utter delight.

So, what happened? Well, with 3FE in hand I resolved to solve two problems with one analytical stone. The best advice a friend and brother gave me is to make your boss happy. Do a good job, the very best job you possibly can, and don't just sit back and wait for them to see you, make yourself seen. Be seen doing what you do. Then, as you take on more responsibility and accountability, work on moving them up and out of the space they currently occupy by making their job that much easier. They'll greatly appreciate it because you're making them look very good, priming them for a promotion to the next level.

The way my friend specifically put it was make them shine. If you make them shine, when you shine, both of you may get what you desire, promotion to the next level. Getting your boss promoted clears a path for you to move into their position, if that's possible. Or, it simply allows you to be more marketable, and transition into another position in the company, or even leave your current company all together for greener pastures elsewhere. Or, perhaps the education the ordeal provides will springboard you into entrepreneurship, and you charting your own way, as your own boss. This is a positive outlook on a potentially very negative situation. It requires a positive attitude, and such a positive attitude is what you must commit to maintaining.

It took me a while to work all this out. To actually get to this point, despite the impending doom just around the corner. I couldn't help but move forward.

I first started with platitudes for my boss, faking positivity. And I mean my manager was making me sick to the very center of my soul. In fact, my manager was making the entire team absolutely ill. Now this was a problem, because my team had very high expectations of me as their leader and supervisor. I was their sword and shield. I was charged with consistently keeping them motivated on top of buffering them from her ire, as the mad-manager with a cold smile from the ninth circle of you-know-where. I was failing going up. And clearly, I was failing going down. But I kept right on walking, right on talking, right on faking.

However, a positive attitude is not something you can fake. It has to be real. Either you have it, or you don't. I spent a couple of weeks languishing in fake positivity, the tool sitting on a bench in the corner of my mind. Then one day, I quite literally stopped, thanks to my wife. You know what she said? She said, *if you come home and consistently talk about this woman, calling her all kinds of names, then you're not addressing the problem. You're not being positive. You're simply trying to deal with the symptom by acting like you're happy. Faking it, is not making it.* I internalized her words.

They truly hit home. I took stock and grabbed the tool off of the mental shelf in the corner of my mind. It was time to actually put the thing to work.

First, I needed to **Find** the issues, given my perspective. I already knew I needed to reprioritize all my tasks, and I do mean all of them. I needed the details on what I was required to accomplish in addition to what my boss needed me to accomplish, and just for clarities sake where some of those tasks might actually lead. My manager had a fondness for assigning phantom tasks that logically made sense to her, and her alone. I would have to think ahead and consider the possibilities, if I was going to make her happy. The only way to achieve this was to suck it up and get closer to her, make her my partner in all things work-related above and beyond what would normally be expected. I needed to converse with her, solicit her opinions, discuss options with her much more frequently than would normally be necessary. I knew this would make her happy, as my manager was the consummate bar-none micromanager, and could not countenance management at a distance.

I scrutinized her. My manager could be passionate. My manager appeared to want to have a good time while working, but the two didn't always coincide. My manager's fun didn't necessarily equate to our terror, but this person didn't seem to know how to make it fun, or just let go and have fun. My manager didn't trust easily. My manager had to be in the know on the smallest possible detail, no matter how insignificant. My manager might say "I didn't need to know," but later on would most certainly need to know. My manager found it incredibly difficult to empower others. There was also the belief in extreme over-communication, to the pain of everyone else on the team.

I wrote down all my observations and assessed them. I took a deep breath, sighing heavily. I was in a bad place people. I needed to get out into the sunshine of better days at work. My **Finding** was done. I needed my job. I needed to regain my positivity. I needed to regain my boss's trust and understanding. So, with my observations in hand, I thought about the situation. The overarching question was clear.

How do I once again become successful?

I **Focused** on this question. I took my observations and studied them. I sat down and went over each detail of each encounter I had with my boss. I went over the encounters I had with my peers. I thought about my relationship with the organization. I took all this under consideration in order to build relationships between the pieces of data I had collected. The relationships would turn into essential information and help me determine my next step.

Well, after all that thinking, all that rumination, all that **Focusing**, I realized my problems really boiled down to a few simple, salient, concise points. I mean, I really leaned back and laughed. Everything came down to a simple exercise. The exercise worked in any given situation, made me responsible and accountable, and held my boss to the same regard. In each of the things I noticed in my **Find** phase I could see that what was broken in between the pieces of information and they could be readily solved by taking a specific set of actions steps. These steps would become the tasks in my next phase, where I established my **Fundamentals.**

I had a conversation with my boss about how our relationship was eroding. I was frustrated. My manager was frustrated and told me directly that if I was promoted I would be a failure as a manager. My manager then followed it up with a statement about counseling. People, my boss essentially threatened me with termination. I had to remain composed and get the conversation on the right track.

Unless you have good corporate political connections, you won't get away from a boss who is bugging the crap out of you, or routing you towards the door, *don't let it hit you where the good Lord split you.* Usually, the only way you can win in this situation is to get another job. Well, I wasn't about to allow that to happen. I'll be honest. I LOVED WHERE I WORKED. I was just having a real difficult problem with my current assignment. I didn't want to work anywhere else.

My boss and I spoke frankly. I told her I needed help prioritizing. I told her the whole team needed help in this regard. Everything on our project was an emergency, and all at the same time (everyone has the same problem, but on our team it FELT magnified times twelve!). My manager could not see how badly people would spin under her. She could not see how dejected people were when they had to interact with her.

That's not true. She saw it. She simply didn't know how to address it, how to change to prevent it. And that, my friends, is the plain truth. She didn't have the tools, the ability to change herself. Now, I didn't tell her this. Some bosses will tell you to be frank and give them candid feedback. This may be true for some bosses. However, know your boss well before doing this. Not all bosses can handle candid feedback. You enter this world of managerial feedback at your own peril. However, if you open your eyes and think critically, you'll know exactly what kind of person you're dealing with. Be certain.

What I did tell her was to stop educating me. She kept wanting to grow me. What she essentially wanted me to do was to manage *like* her. She didn't want to grow me, she wanted to re-engineer me and make me into a managerial clone of her.

She helped me prioritize my tasks. I told her I would work on completing them. She was very big on telling me to lead. Well, what I needed her to do was to be my leader. I didn't need her to keep telling me to be the manager of such and such, and this task, and that tasks. No, I didn't need her to tell me these things because I knew she didn't mean it. It wasn't about the objective for her. It was about communicating the details and repeating the objective incessantly. I had finally come back around to seeing things in the same light as when I first started working for her three years earlier. After our conversation, I must say I was back on track. It took a bit more rumination. I considered it all with a bit more critical cognition, cogitating on what was now appearing to be so incredibly simple. I was now ready.

I was able to isolate my problem with my boss to a few very simple principles. These were the same principles I had utilized when I first started my job:

1. **Communication**
2. **Prioritization**
3. **Low-level task management**

Those were my fundamentals people. I kid you not. It was really just that simple. I had to go back to the basics and remember what kind of boss I was working for. I had to be about telling her everything, all the time, every day. Previously, we had grown into a space where some days I only saw her twice a day. Things were getting done and she was focused on other task, tasks suited to her level.

Now, everything had changed. What did she want? She wanted over-communication to the nth degree. Sometimes, over-communication is essential. Sometimes it erodes and gets in the way. What's critical is knowing when it's necessary. On this assignment, with this boss, it was now clearly a constant requirement. Thanks to 3FE, I was able to put together the necessary steps that were required in order to consistently accomplish this task. I instituted over-communication across the team, with a supporting document that provided them with every detail of each other's current tasks. I called it the Team Task Line Report. The team had clear visibility into each other's activities. The report was updated weekly, often enough daily. We used a critical questioning matrix, utilizing 3FE principles in order to answer any questions on any task or situation before she could ask us about said situation or task. It was an onerous truly unnecessary grind.

But what be might unnecessary for some, is absolutely essential for others. The team was ready and primed for combat. As for me, I took my **Fundamentals** and made them actionable.

Task 1. Assess the To Do List.

Task 2. Mark Completed Tasks.

Task 3. Archive Old Tasks.

Task 4. Add New Tasks.

Task 5. Bold Priorities.

Task 6. Validate Priorities with management.

That's it people. Once it was all laid out all I had to do was **Execute.** That's all to it. The above plan was the result of my **3FE** analysis. And, you want to know something? As long as I followed it, my boss and I were just fine. Whenever I didn't, we were at odds. As I said, eventually we had to part ways. However, doing this re-routed me from the door, saving me from termination, and instead directed me towards a new opportunity, one in which I excelled. Turns out I had the makings of a pretty good manager after all.

I'll tell you, for those of you trying to satisfy a difficult boss, task number six turned out to be the most crucial task on the list. The others you should always be doing to some degree anyway. Good workers do this at some level, though sometimes not with consistency or the help of an app or pen and pad. In this situation I needed strong consistency, and I had to increase my level of communication with my boss tremendously. In all honesty, I should never have stepped away from her. This sense that I was empowered and had the authority to be more independent was the start of my problem. Her attention had been focused laser-like on other things and other people. They were catching it to be sure, while I was safe. When they either bit the dust or simply moved on, her laser beams turned their red energy on me. We fell into a deep dark crevice of animosity.

However, through the ridiculously simple steps I divined through my 3FE exercise I was able to climb out of the crevice. She had already climbed out, and I always wondered if she was hoping to leave my behind. But, I was right there with her, ready to turn things around. By communicating more frequently with my boss about my tasks I was able to prioritize effectively, with her input. I was able to delegate more effectively, because she knew about it. I was able to listen, because she needed to communicate with me as well, if only to express her own angst with a given situation. Things improved tremendously.

3FE in the work place is a powerful tool. As stated it can be the hinge upon which opportunity swings, the doorway to salvation, the foundation for your prosperity. It can beat back negativity and gird you against mounting adversity. You only need the courage to use it. And just so you know, I truly came to love that woman. She truly does mean well. She just … can't see herself. And, she struggles with this issue to this very day. However, as ever, for her I maintain hope. A better life is just one look away.

3FE	**Find ... Focus ... establish the Fundamentals ... Execute!!!** **ISSUE 1: Improving My Relationship With My Boss** **so as to not get fired and get on with my life!**
Find	**Who:** My Boss. SHE IS A FUNCTIONING LUNATIC MICRO-MANAGER FROM THE NINTH CIRCLE OF YOU KNOW WHAT! **What:** I'M ABOUT TO GET FIRED! **Where**: at my job. my job. yes my job. and my home. just everywhere. This is really getting depressing. **When:** I don't know. But I'm concerned that I'm going to be counseled really soon. I myself have explained this to people as being routed to the door. Once you start counseling the writing is on the wall. They're trying to fire you. All I know ... is that it's going to be soon. I can't be certain when. **Why:** If I'm honest I think this is happening because our team structure has changed and the way in which I delegate and communicate does not please her at all. I work through people, and thanks to my skill I can step in at their level and assist where necessary. After the team re-structuring I became her sole focus, and she hated what she saw. **How:** This is occurring because of how the team is structured. It's occurring as we communicate, or fail to communicate. It's happening as she makes up new tasks on the fly, change tasks mid-stream, or just doesn't like the way tasks are accomplished because it's different from how she would have done it.

Focus	**My Boss and our relationship:** There are a number of factors at play here, and I have known about them all along. There is a reason for her behavior, her outlook on life, her control on her emotions, her lack of compassion and her expression of true compassion that seems to be feigned. She is a complex person and very narrowly focused. She can't see herself and how she affects others, and the glimmer of hope she has shown from time to time is just that, only a glimmer. The truth never takes hold. She always KNOWS she's right, no matter the facts that prove otherwise. She has a very narrow perspective.
	Solution. I recognize all of this, and instead of getting angry at it, I have to be accepting of it, and learn to use it to my advantage, and her satisfaction. The only way to do this is to improve our communication to an effective level. I do understand her. Now I must put that knowledge to good use
	I think I'm about to get fired: This is of immediate concern. After having led my team successfully and being awarded for it, I now fear I'm about to be terminated.
	Solution: I need to talk to my HR representative. Not to complain, but just to get her perspective on what's transpiring. If I know my boss, she's probably already been over there getting me set up for the eventual fall. I need to state my position to HR and ensure they know my perspective as well. My boss has an infamous reputation. I don't. I can't allow her to create one for me.
	The work environment: My work environment feels stifling. I dread coming in every day.

Solution: I have to leverage the environment to my benefit. I have to make sure my visibility is appropriate. I have to connect with other Directors and Vice Presidents. And it can't be seen as a plea for help. It must be seen as a strong statement of competent work and effective contribution. I have to make sure there is a marketing effort at work for me in the workplace.

Am I about to be counseled? This is the first step towards termination. I must avoid it at all costs.

Solution: Change how my boss views me. Communication between us must be clear, constant, and consistent. Somehow I have to almost know what she is thinking. The process I leverage must allow me to do this. I have to view the team and our tasks from her perspective. My To Do list has to actually reflect her To Do list. I have to use the team to my advantage and make sure they're on my page in terms of task definitions, completion dates, and what's required to complete the task.

The Power Move: The team structure has changed and she's focused on me. Her power move to eliminate me must be turned into my own power move to excel up and out of her purview.

Solution: I can't turn myself into her, nor do I want to. I have to get her back on an even keel, liking me, and what I do. Then, as everything is quiet, I have to get off the team. I hate to leave them, but I have served my time and must move on.

Fundamentals	The information centers around tasks. Clearly that's what I need to address ... the tasks and how she perceives me accomplishing those tasks. It is absolutely essential that I over-communicate my tasks, and any extra activities associated with those tasks. I have to make my To Do list stay even or one step ahead of her own list. It's an absolute must. The plan is clearly simple. Execution will be tedious, but if I do it, things should get better. **Task 1.** Assess the To Do List. **Task 2.** Mark Complete Tasks. **Task 3.** Archive Old Tasks. **Task 4.** Add New Tasks. **Task 5.** Bold Priorities. **Task 6.** Validate Priorities with management.
Execute	IT'S MONDAY MORNING! Read ... set ... EXECUTE!

My personal experience was really an exercise in essential problem solving and clear thinking. Even though the problem revolved around soft-skills and human interaction, 3FE could still be applied. In order to resolve my crisis I had to step away from the emotion of the situation and focus on the facts with a rational mind. Now, let's go over another use of the tool in the heat of trying to meet the objective and succeed when it's all up to you to get it done, and get it done well.

Daisy Mumford was hired to work at AT&T as a project manager. She was a strong advocate of 3FE and had leveraged the tool several times over the course of her career. She figured this time would be no different. Still, it was hard. The tool could be used iteratively and aggressively, in varying levels of complexity, however it was needed in order to get the job done. This time however life was posing a significant challenge. Aggressive would be the call of the day. And personally, she needed aggressive. It helped to stave off despair.

She was lucky to even get the job given the recession. But she was good and she knew it. Hiring was actually starting to pick up in Information Technology, despite what seemed to be reported on the news every day. She sent a quick prayer up to God, thanking the almighty for the numerous blessings in her life. She then followed it with another prayer for her daily situation. Her faith was powerful and one way or another she knew she would be alright.

The project implementation deadline was set in stone. Project deliverables were falling behind. The functional areas were not working with each other. Management had lost visibility. The person who was on the project before had quit quite suddenly. Daisy was entering a desperate situation at work, after living a desperate situation at home. Her husband had been in a tragic car accident that had almost cost him his life. It had left him nonambulatory for weeks. She had taken time off to care for him, and subsequently lost her previous job. It was a smaller company and had been cutting staff. Though she was highly valued, they had to let her go.

Daisy entered this new project with her eyes wide open. She had been told it was a mess. However, they needed someone who was a fixer. Her energy, her approach, her problem solving skills, had all convinced them she was the one. She had only told them about her husband after she was hired. She felt bad about it, but she really needed the job. She was only human. However, she was ethical and was bound and determined to do what was right. She explained her situation to her boss on her first day, and told him it would in no way impact her ability to do her job. He wasn't pleased, but he was compassionate. He told her he hoped he had not made the wrong decision. Her stomach did backflips, but she held onto faith, and resolved herself to operate as her best self consistently without fail. She now had something to prove. Failure was not an option.

She was hired with one and only one directive. Jump quickly into the deep end of this project, and fix it. That's all. It's just that simple.

Thankfully for Daisy, she had a technical background as a software developer with an emphasis in telecommunications technologies. She knew the technical details of what she managed on her IT projects and was blessed with the ability to tell a developer, tester, configuration manager, or business analyst what side was up, what side was down, and when and where they went wrong, in addition to accurately knowing and rewarding them when they did it right. This was a powerful competitive advantage for Daisy as a project manager, and she leveraged it for maximum effect on all her projects.

Daisy hit the ground running.

She pulled the team together. She had her pad for notes, with rectangles on it. In her head she moved immediately into intense observation mode. There would not be so much talking from her lips, little or none as a matter of fact, a critical question here, a critical question there. She was here to listen. She needed to learn. She engaged the team and set a tone that said I'm here to help, not hinder, to lead as a partner, not a dictator, to seek understanding, and leverage what they bring to the table, and finally be the bridge to success that they needed her to be, resolving the tactical issues of negative conflict by turning them into positive conflict, and defining reasonable solutions. She took a deep breath, thoughts of home never too far away, and started to **Find** out just what in the world was going on.

Turns out the disparate technical teams were very bright, actually they were brilliant. Some of them were clearly too smart for their own good. They lacked direction and cohesion. Objectives conflicted and everyone thought they knew the right thing to do. On top of this, there was no one with the people skills necessary to remove what was clearly nothing more than administrative road-blocks. They lacked executive support, clearly because the executives didn't support them. They saw this as a looming failure that couldn't be allowed to fail. Daisy was really on the firing line.

As she listened to the team, the criticality of what she was dealing with became clearer and clearer. Yes, she was going to have to be aggressive. However, the stone hand she would have to wield would need to be covered in a very soft glove. These brilliant minds needed to see perspective, and bullying them wouldn't get the job done. Actually, bullying never got the job done effectively. When the objective was reached by the hand of a bullying leader, bruised and broken bodies were invariably left in the project's wake, the result of failed leadership. This always resulted in a dysfunctional team. Daisy wondered just how bad the last project manager was.

After that first meeting, with her notes in hand, roles identified, and details broken down to their lower-level constituent components, she went into 3FE overdrive. She took a strategic view of the project and ensured her objectives coincided with long term objectives for the project's success, just to be considerate of what would come next. She then looked at all her available data and made sure she understood the tactical needs that would allow them reach their objective. She identified the area of the project that needed the most hand-holding, making its needs her most immediate priority. She ranked the needs of the other areas, the specific teams, specific tasks that were being held up due to conflicts, administrative action or lack thereof, or just plain confusion. She continued her fact finding, and categorized all the data until she felt she had enough to move forward

She next **Focused** on building relationships between the bits of data, what things had dependencies, what things required help from outside areas. The data became useful information with an almost easy, clearly defined progression path forward towards the objective. She would have to multi-task, but too much multi-tasking led to task quality degradation. You can't focus on twenty things at once. Her prioritization would have to be exceptionally tight, bunching certain tasks together, and delegating what she could to the most trustworthy team leads.

She took another deep breath.

She moved on to establish the **Fundamental** tasks for each of the functional areas. The fundamental tasks become a fundamental plan. Her first priority was the group that was the worst off. She put together a detailed action plan to work with them on firming up their tasks, and getting them organized. She would facilitate their communications, listen to their frustrations, consider their perspectives on why they felt things had completely fallen off the rails. Then, she planned to help them turn towards positivity by facilitating sessions that focused on quickly solving the immediate issues, unwinding the difficult knots of conflict, and identifying the dependencies, addressing them appropriately. In the middle of all this work she decided to solely take on the task of addressing their hardware problem.

The last project manager had not even partnered with the Operations Engineer and Infrastructure Manager to facilitate the purchase of the new hardware they needed. This was ridiculous and inexcusable. Deployment was only two months away.

Once all was completed on her project plan to the lowest details, as such an aggressive plan had to be, she could leave almost nothing to chance; she analyzed her plan quickly, diligently, and critically. She communicated the **Fundamentals** to management in a high level executive meeting. Everything was broken out into a fine Power Point presentation. Each executive had a copy of the presentation in their hands along with supporting materials. She didn't mind the heat in the kitchen. She didn't mind the pressure. She was bound and determined to succeed. She had used the tool for motivational empowerment and felt powerfully motivated.

After her presentation there was silence … and then, smiles. No applause as such. No standing ovations. All they had was a plan, something they had wanted desperately, but success, the objective, was still weeks away. They wouldn't know if they had gotten their money's worth by hiring Daisy until the day the project went live. However, for now they were in firm approval of her actions, and the plan she laid before them. All that was needed, was permission to pull the trigger … and they gave it.

Daisy Executed.

She did this 3FE exercise in an iterative nature, at different levels, for each of her functional areas. By employing 3FE, she remained motivated, even if sometimes she did feel stressed. She felt good about overcoming the challenges, and digging into the details. 3FE helped her dig into those details, and put together an effective plan. By iteratively examining her plans across her functional areas, she was able to remain ahead of changes, and deal with any obstacles that cropped up. In the end, the project was incredibly successful. For her efforts she received an award and a permanent home with the company. More importantly, she earned the respect and trust of her entire team. They all, down to a man and woman took the time to thank her for her efforts, for leading them well, for unraveling the mess they had become, and for guiding them to success.

The accolades humbled her greatly. She didn't seek the recognition. Her journey with 3FE had turned her into a powerful critical thinker, not only in her job, but in her home life as well. She now had an assured path with the company that would lead to promotion. This was all good, a story that culminated with the financial security she so desperately needed. She had to share the entire experience with her husband, who was doing much, much better. Yes, for Daisy … life had indeed turned out to be quite good.

3FE	**Find ... Focus ... establish the Fundamentals ... Execute!!!** **ISSUE 1: Save the Project From Doomsday** **Over-arching 3FE Analysis**
Find	**Who:** It's twofold. Me, in terms of successfully securing a position as the new project manager. And the team, in terms of their total dysfunction. The team is broken into functional areas, and the areas are in constant negative conflict with each other. **What:** I've got to get educated quickly. This is going to require a multi-pronged approach. I have to understand the problem, and the solution we're delivering. I have to listen to each area and determine what they're responsible for. Then, I have to bring them all back together focusing on the goal. **Where**: In the building the teams are located in different areas. I need to carve out neutral ground in order to bring them together. However, to start, I need to go to each area lead, speak to them on their turf, get their perspective, internalize it, understand where there are coming from. **When:** There is very little consideration for time. The deadline is hard and fast, only a few months away. I'll have to work around the clock each and every week. This will include the weekends. I have to establish daily milestones, starting with my focused approach to getting educated.

	Why: I have to understand the whys of why this team is failing. That will come from good listening, and good partnering. My initial assessment is it's simply a lack of leadership and territorial infighting. Effective communication and support will address this issue.
	How: The process is paramount. I have to start with listening. Gain an understanding of why we're here, but there isn't a lot of time for this activity. As I listen I have to start angling them towards being more solution-oriented. I need them to switch gears and start working as a unit on the one objective. Responsible not only to themselves, but to each other. My leadership skills will be tested thoroughly.
Focus	**Me:** I have to be firm. My life has become very difficult. I have skirted the ethical line, which is a powerful disappointment. But I needed this job in the worst way. Now that I have it, I have to make them see that hiring me was the absolute right choice. I can do that by leveraging all the tools at my disposal and use them effectively on a daily basis. I have to put together my new To Do list.
	Team: The leads are some of the smartest people in the building. They are also very arrogant, and narrow in vision. They're too busy looking at themselves and can't readily see the big picture.
	Solution: My To Do list is absolutely critical to my success. I'm working on it immediately. I'm going to have two hour long sessions with each functional area over the course of the next two days. I'm going to listen. Then, I'm going to speak with each team lead and explain to them what we need to do to succeed … starting with the understanding that we need a little more WE and a lot less ME

Schedules: The teams are not managing their time. They're disjointed and totally out of focus. They have no idea what's coming next, and apparently don't care to plan for it. That's all about to change.

Solution: I'm going to start with the project schedule outline that the company supplies. I need to identify the weekly milestones and daily milestones. Then, I need to break out my sub-schedules for these tactical tasks that I need in each functional area. I'm going to delegate some of this to the leaders in each team. I need to manage through them, not for them.

Building the team: These teams and these individuals are not inclined to work together. Their dysfunction is all about who is responsible for what, and who feels important. They have no management support and they know it, and now I'm understanding they think they don't need it. They lack leadership and lack the ability to provide it for themselves. They're failing and failing rapidly.

Solution: I'm scheduling listening and learning sessions. I'm getting with the leaders. Then, I have to get them with each other. They have to understand what each of them do, and why they are important to each other, and the project. I have to get educated on their conflicts and then educate them on what the true reasons are behind their conflicts, removing the negative, but preserving the ability to engage each other in positive conflict, thereby divining answers that serve both themselves, and the project … and hopefully me.

Fundamentals	**Task 1:** Create initial Project Manager To Do list with all the necessary detail. **Task 2:** Schedule a meeting with the team leads (a change from my original plan). **Task 3:** Schedule group meeting with combined teams. **Task 4:** Schedule morning stand-up meetings with combined team leads. **Task 5:** Schedule breakout focus sessions with functional areas. **Task 6:** Establish communication protocol. **Task 7:** Document all details and tasks from sessions. **Task 8:** Build project schedules and tasks lists. **Task 9:** Address admin issues and operational concerns personally due to time constraints (put it on my To Do List and partner with Operations teams). **Task 10:** Put together presentation for aggressive approach. **Task 11:** Present approach to upper management with expectation that we will be allowed to proceed forward. **Task 12:** STAY CONSISTETNLY POSITIVE AND UPBEAT ... STAY STEADY ON THE GRIND!
Execute	Phase 1: Execute immediate action plan above. Phase 2: Execute subsequent plans from lower level 3FE analyses. Phase 3: Execute the above action plan and present progress on a weekly basis to upper management.

To close this chapter I'm going to present you now with an essay I wrote once upon a time. It describes the utilization of 3FE and the critical thinking mindset within a fluid job setting. We need not, or rather absolutely cannot shut down the essential apparatus of our critical thinking mind. We must engage in a true effort to evolve into better thinkers. This cannot occur if we only apply the critical thinking mindset to a specific set of circumstances. No, we must always embrace the critical thinking mindset, and when appropriate we can reach for the tool for motivational empowerment in order to break down a more complex concept, understand it more thoroughly, and then solicit opinion, or define a course of action.

Well, monkey in the middle.

The meeting was definitely on the skids, sliding left or right, take your pick, but it was definitely off track, and dissolving into complete chaos. Is that you in the above picture? Look, it's a monkey with a pen in his mouth. Is he about to make a decision, a decision that has completely and totally pissed you off? Do you look at your boss and see a monkey in a tie? Is this how you feel? Is it sending you into a tailspin, down through several layers of mental chaos? Is your world spinning out of control? Is this how you view some of your peers, your boss, your boss's boss? Is this a constant thing or just something that arises from time to time, mostly within the realm of the emergency issue, when the project is in red status, or real-world production operations have floundered and threaten to impact the customer directly, as in monetarily, in the pocket so to speak. Is this the mental state of mind for you and your team when in the midst of chaos? Do you not only see monkeys, but descend into chaos, thinking no better than an untrained monkey? Well, to begin with, don't insult the monkey.

If you are a leader, first you mist dismiss the above image. See NO MONKEYS … unless you work at a zoo.

So, you're in chaos. So, you're struggling. So, your management has started to play out a scenario from a Dilbert cartoon. The question becomes how will you deal with the situation? What options do you have? What's your approach? Can you lead, at least yourself, out of this chaos?

The answer is always yes. There are always options.

And let me be perfectly clear, every person should aspire to be a leader, even if it means the only person you're leading is yourself. Let us start with the understanding that applying 3FE requires introspection and a commitment to viewing yourself as reaching for leadership within your own sphere of influence. If the only person you're leading is yourself, then lead yourself with spirit and vigor, lead yourself effectively!

How do you control the chaos? How do you harness its power? Through the utilization of the tool for motivational empowerment you can learn to readily harness the power of your mind to relax and breathe, concentrate effectively, apply a critical thinking approach, and get control of even the most complex situations.

Let me share a brief story.

I arrived at work on a fine Tuesday morning and joined a conference call. The subject was the urgent mitigation of a risk that was threatening to become a major issue to our project. The issue, if not handled effectively could conceivably derail the entire project, costing us hundreds of thousands of dollars. Needless to say, this was an unacceptable outcome.

The manager in charge of this enterprise-level project described the overall situation and proceeded to detail the three options that were on the table to resolve the issue. After a few moments, one of our more vocal Vice Presidents chimed in. His first question brought the entire conference call to a halt. From there, the conference call seemed to descend into chaos.

You could feel the tension building through the electronic lines. Many of you have experienced this before. A conference call where it feels quite painful, where you wonder what's going to be said next, where if you're in a room with someone you both look at each other with wide eyes, and one of you may say, *that's really bad!*

I was alone in my office. In my mind's eye I saw the other Vice Presidents on the line cringing, Directors squirming, my fellow managers bending under perceived pressure. My Supervisor spoke up, trying to bring the call back on course. The Vice President listened, and then continued where he left off. The call ended with people taking action items and an understanding that we want to do the right thing, but the right thing was clouded by nervousness, a lack of direction, and a fear of chaos, chaos that could doom the entire project at a critical juncture.

Before moving forward let's put the conversation in proper context. Understand, I did not provide the specific details of the dialogue because in this exercise of understanding they truly aren't necessary. My point is to give you a general understanding of the chaos generated on the call, and how I effectively took the data available and developed a fundamental approach, a plan to execute within my area of responsibility, and outside it where I was able.

On the call, in specific, even as I listened, mentally I was forcing my mind forward, breaking through the static, and preparing to act. I was forcing myself through a focused multi-level mental activity, finding and mentally highlighting the essential details of the issue, and weighing the political implications of possible actions that were clarified on the conference call.

First things first, a holistic mental approach in this Find phase is essential. What are the things we wish to Find? What details around the facts of the issue help us cut through the chaos and derive order? We understand that this VP is a minority. Despite the progress made with regard to minorities in the workplace, there remain challenges, challenges that a minority may perceive from his perspective, some of which may not be factual, and some that are most certainly quite real. To that end, as a result of being very effective, this particular VP had developed a reputation. He is even feared. His manner, and powerful voice, which cuts through minutia and gets straight to the point is the source of consternation and legendary fear. However, what did he say on this call? What was he trying to accomplish? What did he truly say? I focused on his words. I parsed them. He was simply trying to make sure we took the requisite time and utilized due diligence in how we resolved the issue. He was trying to get us to do the right thing. That's all. His delivery of this request struck many on the call as heavy-handed. However, I'm fairly certain much of this perception was a function of his doing the delivery. In other words, the perception is flawed, not factual at all.

With this data and basic understanding, I quickly detailed the people with whom I needed to converse. I detailed a list of possible options for action. I divined what my superiors might want to know and put together an essential action plan that would be highly effective within whatever action my superiors deemed necessary. My most important task was to diffuse the emotions and chaos and elevate options. I knew I would need to make sure my people were prepared to do one thing with many facets … answer questions and critically consider multiple possibilities.

From the perceived disaster of the conference call I defined my quick action plan, which was essentially walking, talking, directing, and delegating. I was well on my way, when my phone rang. It was my boss. He had remained silent on the call, and he was clearly taken aback. I think what he was feeling was a result of the perceived chaos on the call, again a function of perception with regard to who was delivering the message.

We spoke briefly, and he gave me some marching orders, all of which fit nicely within the framework of what I was already intending to do. When utilizing 3FE effectively you'll find that those who exhibit critical thinking skills in action will most certainly say and do things similar to what you are planning. It is as though you are in synch. Why? Simple, because the path to resolution is logical, and if you're not too lost in the chaos, you can both readily see the way out.

To make a long story short I quickly met up with my peers and reports. Bits and pieces of what we needed to do were already being stated. Again, problem solving logically, readily lends itself to the 3FE methodology, and if others are trying to solve the issue using critical thinking skills, they will naturally fall in line.

I quickly stated my 3FE approach, which I detail below and requested an immediate meeting with the appropriate people in order to get us the facts, with possible options for consumption by our superiors. Getting the appropriate parties in a room is always an important consideration, and 3FE still applies. When in the meeting, adhere to the methodology in order to effectively resolve the issue. How did we proceed?

FIND
Quickly assess the conference call.
Identify the chaos and any data around it that might be pertinent.
What is the core issue and any associated variables?

FOCUS
Focus on the details from the call.
Diffuse the chaos, which was simply a function of emotion, an emotive response.
Clarify the issue and look at what's critical with regard to the issue.
Ask the critical questions as to what it is and how we can possibly resolve it.
Take the data and make it into meaningful information.

establish the FUNDAMENTALS
The focused information will give rise to relationships among various tasks.
Take the tasks and assign them to resources for completion.
Establish completion dates for each task.
Identify the milestone dates that represent important steps towards resolution.
Determine the effective completion date.

EXECUTE
Once the plan has been established Execute it.
Understand that risk and issues don't go away.
Mitigate risks and address issues.

If you fail, assess and re-execute with the express purpose of attaining the objective.

I utilize the power of 3FE every day for any given problem that impacts my sphere of influence. I highly recommend you do the same, if only to exercise your mind in preparation for what is, and what can possibly be.

The power of 3FE is motivating and empowering by its very nature. I felt motivated in understanding the situation quickly from multiple standpoints because I listened intently, I asked critical questions, I focused on the information and clearly recognized a natural order for action that was readily derived from the available data. I focused on doing that which made sense. I established my Fundamental Plan, got up from behind my desk, and I Executed. In the meeting, I continued to Execute.

Business moves at the speed of thought, and to make the speed of your work move at an effective velocity fit for the overall journey you must utilize critical thinking skills. Your thoughts must be constructed in such a manner as to have taken into consideration the discernable facts, the data. That data must become focused, paying particular attention to the pertinent facts and the various implications inherent in the data both tactical and strategic. From that data comes information, elevated and understood, defining a clear and concise path forward crafted into a fundamental plan, one that is emphatic with clearly defined milestones, and an overarching objective. Your plan must be appropriately replete with the requisite detail. It must be complete in terms of effectiveness. When it is ready, then you are ready. Pull the trigger! Execute! Execute! Execute!

Chapter 6

LOCK THE JOB!

You want a job.

A simple statement that in harsh economic times translates to you need a job, you need a job so bad that every day you feel yourself slipping closer to the edge of the cliff. You fear the fall and no one seems to care. You fear the fall and your desperation increases. You fear the fall so greatly that you may even consider doing something unsavory to survive, because it's more than just making ends meet, juggling one bill for another. In the coming months, you wonder how you're going to eat. You wonder how you're going to live.

Can I guarantee you a job?

I could say after a fashion, yes. Or, I can be emphatic and say without equivocation that I can guarantee you a job. Yes, I'm going to be emphatic. I CAN AND WILL GUARANTEE YOU A JOB! I will freely make this statement because what I am about to offer you is the key to the kingdom of employment and prosperity. However, this guarantee only applies if you follow these guidelines specifically to the letter. Deviations only apply as dependent to the situation. For instance, you may join a different type of networking group to help you achieve your objective, such as WIT Women in Technology, or NAIFA the National Association of Insurance & Financial Advisors, or IIBA the International Institute of Business Analyst.

In order to push this guarantee more effectively I have put together an approach called 3FE: Lock The Job, which utilizes what I call the Red Resume process and other differentiating concepts in order to Find the areas necessary to promote your personal brand, Focus on what you need to do in order to differentiate yourself in the market, establish your Fundamental approach for finding a job, and Executing on this approach with maximum effect.

I teach this because I feel it is absolutely necessary. In the 21st century, as the truth becomes clear that only two things create jobs, innovation and demand, each person will need to recognize their value and determine how best to brand themselves in a market that may very well become saturated, or as it is now for Information Technology, experiencing a shortage.

There is a dearth of available American talent in Information Technology. Companies have ever increasing needs as innovation on top of innovation enters the market. However, at the same time when the need is being met there is a glut of talent clamoring for the same job. How do you avoid having to go through five interviews? How do you distinguish yourself from your competition? How do you brand yourself so that you blow them away the moment they look at your resume? How do you explode through the vetting process? How do you convince the recruiter to lobby for you? How do you wow them in the interview such that you are the only person they consider? How do you lock the job from Day 1?

This challenge can exist in any line of employment. Whether you work in Information Technology, Retail, Healthcare, or Manufacturing, what are the factors that you must highlight? What story must you tell about yourself to ensure that you stand out from the crowd in a way that makes you the prime candidate, the obvious choice, the one who locks the job?

Below I will provide a real world example of the type of guidance 3FE provides. I will introduce you to Lock the Job, and the Red Resume concept by showing you what 3FE offers, and how if utilized as prescribed, it most assuredly helps you reach your objective, get the position you desire, LOCK THE JOB.

Thomas Trane had worked hard to achieve his goals and motivate himself to be the best that he could be. In order to accomplish his goals he has held many menial jobs. He has overcome challenges and been persistent in pursuing his own future. His dedication to the task was initially shown through his move from Oklahoma to Atlanta. He moved in an effort to secure a position in his chosen field of Information Technology. This is something to be applauded. It's not easy for some people to just pick up and move, leave behind everything they've ever known and start off new in another city, with no certainty of employment. Thomas knew Atlanta was a better job market. He figured his chances in Atlanta would be far better than Tulsa, Oklahoma. He moved on faith.

 Just to be clear, Thomas's educational achievement has surpassed most people in his age group. This is no trite statement. Despite what people say I firmly believe educational achievement remains of high value, and college degrees are not to be marginalized. They have meaning. In my opinion this is not something to be taken lightly. This is truth, and truth branded as such, carries weight. A degree in IT, though not at all a requirement, can add inestimable value if utilized appropriately. Thomas had achieved a Bachelor's and Master's degree and he remained dedicated to his chosen field. He wanted to grow in IT.

 But for Thomas this was just the beginning of the story, a good beginning, but like any story there were ups and downs.

 He was growing weary of the grind. He had pushed and pushed and pushed, and he was more than a bit tired of the search for employment. Whether it was the truth or a fallacy, the perception one had upon meeting him was that he was almost done, as though he were a car that was rapidly running out of gas. However, he still had the desire to achieve. He wanted to work in his field. He had reached a lofty height on the mountain thanks to his education, but had yet to make it to the mountaintop. He wanted greatly to be the man standing on the mountaintop.

 Thomas Trane had a great deal of energy and a sincere desire to do the right thing. He wanted to support himself and be totally self-sufficient. However, like many in his generation he had a somewhat skewed perspective on society. He thought someone, somewhere owed him something. He genuinely felt society owed him a job. Now, he didn't think it would be given freely. He simply felt that he'd worked hard, earned his degrees, and now the rest should be easy. He believed he should be granted a boon, given a job for earning good grades. He believed this as did many of his friends. Now, this is not a generalization. His generation as one monolithic group does not necessarily share this perspective. However, some of them do, and for the goal of attaining employment, this perspective presents itself as a serious impediment to success.

Unless Thomas saw the world as it truly was and recognized that no one owed him anything, he would not succeed. He first had to recognize that as an intelligent able-bodied man he must first stand strong on his own two feet, and accept the fact that he would only receive help if he helped himself first … which meant helping himself to a good helping of additional work in the field, trying to isolate the job that fit his skill set, and doing what was necessary to secure it.

He had to recognize that even as he did this he could find and receive help, outstanding help, but the help he got may not be exactly what he wanted. However, it would most likely be exactly what he needed. He alone had the power to truly choose for himself.

Thomas had resigned himself to staying at home and asking for help from his mother. She sent him a check every week. He used to work at what he called menial jobs, but after getting his Master's degree he saw menial jobs as beneath him. He felt the world owed him better. He saw no point in working a cash register, or stocking shelves. He felt he was better than that, now that he was appropriately educated. He felt really, really bad about leaning on his mother for money, but he was not about to stoop down and go menial. He was not about to take a job beneath him. He just knew the world owed him better, and he was bound and determined to sit … and wait.

This, was of course absolutely unacceptable.

First, Thomas had to undergo a change in mindset. This required some tough love from the people he engaged when he moved to Atlanta. Even as they continued to give him positive encouragement they made it clear to him that people who were hungry, people who didn't mind sweeping streets, cutting grass, dropping fries, cooking burgers, or cleaning toilets would be viewed far better by prospective employers when compared to someone who had been sitting on his backside waiting for someone to give him a job. It took several conversations for Thomas to realize this truth, but he finally got it. Not only did he get it, but he understood the truth of it internally. Being a stock boy or dropping fries was not beneath him by any stretch of the imagination. In fact, being willing to spend hours working, and then additional hours searching for a job in his chosen field was quite honorable. It was the right thing to do.

He may think he is doing all he can, but he is not. Thomas must first do all he can do in order to secure employment right now! He needs to get a job today! He must start with gainful employment no matter what it is. That is the driving force that will get him to the next level. But first he must be responsible. He must be accountable. He must own his situation, and that starts by going out and getting a job, NO MATTER WHAT!

Thomas has two degrees! Thomas has a Masters degree. Thomas has a 3.5 GPA! THOMAS IS NEAR THE END OF THE FIRST ROAD BUT HE MUST JUMP ONTO THE HIGHWAY. We don't want him to miss the on-ramp. What does this require? It requires that Thomas remain positive, that he does not quit no matter what. Thomas must embrace critical thinking and use the power of his mind to resolve his problem, and do what he knows he can in his heart, secure gainful employment in his chosen field at a level that rewards his hard work with good compensation, work-life balance, and overall satisfaction. He can do this. But, he must be a critical thinker.

3FE	Find ... Focus ... establish the Fundamentals ... Execute!!! **ISSUE 1: Getting a Job**
Find	**Who:** Thomas Trane. **What:** Needs to get a job ... he wants to get a job as a Project Manager. **Where:** Here in Atlanta. There are over 5000 open IT jobs, but the work starts with getting a job, any job, not just an IT job. **When:** As soon as possible. **Why:** He needs to seek gainful employment in his field urgently. **How:** Circumstance has created this situation but it is not the fault of anyone in particular. In order to secure a job in his field in a demand increasing environment he must stand out. Differentiation is the absolute key to success.
Focus:	**Thomas Trane:** Thomas needs to do some soul searching and have a very powerful conversation with himself. Self-conversations, literal conversations with the mirror can prove to be very effective and powerful. **Solution:** Be a leader in your own space. BE A LEADER, NOT A FOLLOWER! This will require that you make no excuses, expect nothing from anyone, and beg for nothing. You have to demand what you want from this world, but in order to get it you must be willing to take action. NO ONE WILL GIVE YOU ANYTHING, AND NO ONE OWES YOU ANYTHING.

GET A JOB STARTING TODAY!

Solution: Your resume needs some work, but in its current form it can be used to gain employment at the level required PRIOR to securing a job in IT. A recommendation is the local electronics store, or any job that is still close to technology. Investigate entry level jobs at Greenlight, or other tech companies. The point is to get a job, any job, and be employed WHILE looking for a job.

You can get a job that works a swing shift so you can go on interviews during the day. You might only have the job for 2 to 3 months. One never knows. But certainly people will be much more impressed by someone who has a job, even in a slowly improving economy, than one who feels entitled to a job because he has a degree. However, while you have that job, you can pay your own bills and use that money to execute the steps stated below.

FOCUSING ON IMPROVING THE PICTURE – THE PATH TOWARDS GETTING A JOB REQUIRES MAJOR PREPARATION!

As an IT candidate seek to Join an organization like **BDPA** (https://www.bdpa.org), **TechLatino** (https://techlatino.org/career-center/), **Wireless Technology Forum** (https://wtf20.com) , **Technologists of Color** (https://techsofcolor.org), **or CompTIA** (https://www.comptia.org)

Solution: BDPA has established its first liaison program with Devry. Thomas, you need to be a part of this initiative. You need to not only be a participating member of the program, which means never missing meetings, and committing to completing all activities, you must strive to be a leader as well. You must join BDPA to build out your personal network and create new opportunities.

In BDPA and any other professional organization, you must build your network by joining committees and working on projects with others. Collaboration and teamwork are the very heart of successful Project Management. If you can't work well in a team you can't be a project manager. You must seek out team opportunities in these service organizations in order to make a strong mark that differentiates you and helps address to some degree your lack of experience.

Join The MBA (Masters of Business Administration) Association and/or the NBMBAA (National Black MBA Association)

Solution: This will expand your personal network. Remember, build a network, leverage a network, create an opportunity. You'll build connections through these organizations that you can leverage.

Create a New Resume

Solution: Thomas, your resume is nice, but it must be better. PUT SOME COLOR IN IT … LITERALLY!!! Rework your resume in order to show off your talents. Google Project Management Resumes for some examples. Differentiate yourself. Only resumes that stand out attract attention. The others get tossed to the side in the stacks and stacks go in the trash.

Create a Visual Resume

Solution: Thomas, you absolutely must create a visual resume. This has quickly become a standout mode of self-expression. Check out Slideshare's visual resumes

Your visual resume can be posted to Vimeo, YouTube and LinkedIn, and must be on your professional website, which we discuss next.

Create a website and/or blogsite (Worpress)

Solution: Thomas, you must have your own website. It must have your professional and personal interests, and it must show in a creative way how you went about doing your project work. Since you have no work experience your work must be from school, and eventually those service organizations. DO NOT MENTION IT WAS FROM SCHOOL! There's no need to advertise your lack of professional experience. Let the work speak for itself. Don't feed any preconceived notions.

Create a robust LinkeIn Profile (copy the best style that you find)

Solution: Thomas, you need to build your online profile in LinkedIn. Your profile must list all the information from your resume, as well as information from your website. There must be links, and it must list all the organizations you belong to. Your LinkedIn profile should have your visual resume as well as books you've read on professional development. If you haven't read any books, then you must read them, and read them now. List at least two books on project management that you have read and internalized.

Recreate your professional character

Solution: Thomas at home and Thomas at work can share many of the same characteristics, but the two must be different when it comes to being perceived as the next best thing to hit the work-force. Thomas, you must learn to imitate successful people, and there is a ready-made plan to accomplish this.

- Imitate two professionals as practice to guide your growth. For you in particular I highly recommend Wes Moore and Van Jones. Read both of their books. Watch videos of them on YouTube. This is not a joke, something comical, or something you can blow off. This is the work. This is something you do in order to educate yourself on how you appear. Imitation is the most sincere form of flattery and the best way to grow your engaging self. It is not about denying your true self. It's about unearthing your true professional self, unless that person does not exist. This is work to create your opportunities, if you would choose to do so.

- Let's be honest with ourselves Thomas. You do not sound professional, and your grammar needs some work. Be positive. Be upbeat. Be engaging. And still be you! Understand there is nothing wrong with sounding more WHITE! YES, I SAID IT! INDEED I DID! This is not at the expense of your Blackness. This is about being clearly understood, not about changing who you are to be accepted. If you were Latin, I would say even out your accent as best as you can taking care to limit colloquialisms and slang. If you were Anglo, Irish, Italian-American or down Deep South Redneck with the WHITEST COUNTRY BACKWOODS SLANG I would tell you the same where it was appropriately applicable. People are finicky, and they judge readily. Learn to see them and be prepared to present what works best for the given role. DO IT AND MAKE IT YOURS!

- Watch YouTube videos of Van Jones and Wes Moore. Spend thirty minutes a day for three weeks acting like them, sounding like them, trying to dress like them. Watch the videos closely so you can try to glean how they respond to questions. Essentially, you want to learn from how they present themselves, and evolve your own distinct professional self. You will become your own professional Thomas by acting and learning from Wes and Van, incorporating some of what makes them standout and making it your own.

- At BDPA, and other professional organizational meetings always be in your Wes Moore, Van Jones mode. Do not be in any other mode. Be your professional character and stick to it. You'll know when you can let your guard down, but only after you have become comfortable as Professional Thomas (not a doubting Thomas, scared Thomas, or any other kind of Thomas).

- WORK ON YOUR ELEVATOR SPEECH!

Perfect your Elevator Speech

Solution: Your elevator speech is you in thirty seconds to two minutes of lightning! No more, no less. Spend the next few weeks perfecting your speech. Practice it in the mirror while you're talking to yourself.

Perfect your AE(Anti-Elevator) Speech

Solution: I'm a member of Toastmasters and I recently read an article by member Cliff Suttle. The article detailed how to build a relationship in 10 seconds as opposed to selling yourself in 30 seconds. The point is to deliver a hook, an enticement, something that makes people curious. Cliff uses the hook, "We excite audiences." This is his answer when someone asks what he does for a living. It invites more questions. Google Anti-Elevator speech and consider the AI speech vs. the standard Elevator speech. Be prepared to do both!

Secure Project Management Certification

Solution: You can't get Project Management Certification without actual work experience. However, this should still remain one of your foremost goals. AND while you are at it I highly suggest you get certified in Agile Development as a SCRUM master. Move towards the future.

Join PMI (Project Management Institute) and get your CAPM certification. Pay for it with money from your new job. YES, THE NEW JOB WHERE YOU'RE STOCKBOY, OR WORKING ON FRIES! Then look into getting your PMI certification.

Join Toastmasters

Solution: Look up and join your local Toastmaster's organization. This organization is perfectly suited to boost your character through communication and leadership. It is a *must-participate* organization for people who seek to lead:

	Get with an IT Recruiting company

Solution: Investigate job placement through Matrix Resources, Kelly, Capricorn, TEKSystems, etc. Sign up with one of these companies as a possible path to securing a job.

The Power Move: ONLY AFTER YOU HAVE UPDATED YOUR RESUME, VISUAL RESUME, LINKEDIN PROFILE, WEBSITE, JOINED at least one of the following organizations (BDPA, CompTIA, MBAA, NBMBAA), and PMI, and then spent at least 4 weeks working on your character, being positive, and changing your voice, will you be ready. Then, hit the JOB FAIRS! Present yourself. Pass out your dynamic resumes and let them have it with everything you have to offer. Make them understand that they will be missing out on a GREAT thing if they don't seek to hire you.

Solution: Check out some of the companies listed below, and pull your power move on them:

Ceridian, HP, UPS Logistics, McKesson, Southern Company, Truist, Chik Fi La, AGCO, Delta Airlines, E&Y, PriceWaterHouse Coopers, The Home Depot, Coca Cola, Georgia Tech, Georgia State, Deloitte, Taco Bell. |
| Fundamentals | The information from the above Focus section provides the details for your specific action plan. Execute it to the letter. Execution will at times feel tedious, but if you do it, if you commit to it, things will get better. |

	Task 1. Build my To Do List. My To Do list consists of each task identified in the above Focus section. These things can be broken down into smaller tasks, that I have to do in order to get each job done, and secure my IT employment. **Task 2.** Put completion dates next to each task. **Task 3.** Review the task list and validate it on a daily basis.
Execute	IT'S MONDAY MORNING! Read ... set ... EXECUTE!

Chapter 7

3FE For The Future Entrepreneur

So you think you're a businessman! Put it out there with emphasis. Provide some strength to the statement. If you believe it, and you have the blood to drive the sweat and you're willing to shed tears, then perhaps you do have what it takes, and you are one of those who can step outside and define your own future, chart your own path, pursue your own dream. Perhaps, just perhaps, you are an entrepreneur.

3FE was developed in conjunction with another rule that I consider a mandate for those that think critically and pursue the objective of personal excellence with passion. This objective clarifies one of the paramount goals for the enterprising individual. It is only superseded in critical consideration by the creation and cultivation of relationships with real and true people, as opposed to those people involved in the creation of your personal wealth and the accumulation of material things, which includes the possible creation of a legacy that may well benefit your progeny but will give you little satisfaction in death. I mention this because it's important to put this pursuit in proper perspective, especially in relation to the other rule, the other personal mandate.

What is Critical Success?

Critical Success is the planned achievement of something urgent and essential utilizing careful planning and judgment for the express purpose of attaining personal prosperity. In my book, Critical Success: The 2 Rules of 3, I defined the first rule of 3, which is the subject of this book, 3FE: Find, Focus, establish the Fundamentals, and Execute. The second rule of 3 is 3POP, the 3 Principles of Prosperity. What do the 3 Principles demand of you? The first principle demands that you 1 invest in the Capital Markets. Despite the volatility of the stock market and the fear it generates in the everyday citizen, you must use some of your money to invest in the markets. Over time, you will be rewarded for your perseverance and courage. The second principle demands that you invest in Real Estate, and that does not mean your house. Your house is where you live. Invest in the temporary ownership of land. I say temporary because despite our human laws, the earth belongs to the Earth, and we all need to learn to respect it, and responsibly share it. We are stewards, not owners. The third principle demands that you attempt to start a business, that you try your hand at becoming an entrepreneur. Now recognize that all three principles are not for everyone. We're not all cut out to be entrepreneurs. However, if you can see it, if you can build a fundamental plan that allows you to execute it, with room to pursue such a dream without becoming totally destitute, then GO FOR IT! Give it a shot. Some of you have the wherewithall all to put it all on the line. This for you is a do or die proposition. You have the passion and desire to risk it all. It's all relative … to who we are, and whether or not we truly know ourselves, recognizing our limits as well as our capabilities.

So, the 3rd principle in 3POP is what this chapter is about, and how we might leverage the 1st rule of 3 in order to achieve it. The objective is to be a successful entrepreneur. In order to achieve this objective we will apply the tool for motivational empowerment. Allow me to explain how we might do this with an example.

The objective is to open a restaurant.

We'll use a restaurant in our example because it is truly a favorite. People are always talking about opening up a restaurant or bar. So, let's consider what's required, what it might take, and how one might go about pursuing this objective effectively with the help of 3FE. We'll start with Day 1.

You know what you want to do. You grabbed a piece of paper

ready to engage the methodology. You've given it a considerable amount of thought. Now, you think you're ready. Now, you want to lay down the plan. However, you recognize the need to plan, the need to think critically, to fully leverage the 1st rule of 3 in achieving critical success and adhere to the 3rd principle of the 2nd rule of 3 in achieving critical success. You have a pencil in your hand. A piece of paper is on the table in front of you. You're ready. You draw rectangles, and then proceed in earnest.

3FE	Find ... Focus ... establish the Fundamentals ... Execute!!! **I'M OPENING THE SOUTH'S HOTTEST SOUL FOOD RESTAURANT/CAFE**
Find	**Who:** Mainly me. However, I want to get my nephew to help, and my Aunt who has my grandmother's best recipes. **What:** Restaurants fail all the time. I am committed to making my restaurant successful! **Where**: I'm investigating. I have a few good spots. I've learned about the location rule. Location, location, location is absolutely important and this will require a thorough analysis. **When:** I'm giving myself a year for thorough analysis and preparation, and an additional six months for buildout and opening day. I can't rush this. **Why:** I have a dream, a passion for food. I know my food is delicious and I want to share it. People tell me I should open a restaurant all the time. I'm not as ignorant as I once was, I know this isn't easy.

	How: Everyone has an idea on how to do this. There are a ton of plans out there. I'm going to use 3FE to get this done, leverage the best of breed and learn what good restaurant owners do. The How for me will be my CRITICAL PLAN!
Focus	**Me, what am I bringing to the table:** I have an idea. But I need a plan. I need to focus on what's required to open a restaurant first, and a very successful one. I need the fundamental building blocks. I need to think about who I know, and who can help me. I have to do a lot of reading. I know reading is absolutely fundamental. I know in order to do something right I have to do the proper research. I already took a course at a community college on writing a business plan and a marketing plan. I've made quite a few friends that have done some research and can help me find the answers I need. I've got some family members who can help. What I need is my team, with me thinking ahead all the time as the leader. • My task list • My team • My funds situation • The business plan • Focused research • Innovation all by itself is important. My plan to make myself distinctive is critical. (The band venue, the deck, the mixed drinks, the Black Southern Art, and the alcoholic coffee) **Solution:** There is a great deal of research that needs to be done. I need to prioritize the research. I need to identify the candidates for my team. I need to really

think about funding. I'll develop my prioritized task list and schedule of activities. This will keep me organized and focused.

Restaurants Fail: I need to understand the why's of this failure. This is absolutely critical, and I know people fail at this all the time. They never take the time to understand why restaurants that look like they're doing good fail.

Solution: If I'm going to be successful I need to write a report on why restaurants fail, and understand it completely, so I can avoid it.

Restaurant Location: I'll need to do even more research here. I've got a place where I would like to open my restaurant. However, I've seen too many times where the perfect spot turns out to not be the perfect spot. I need to understand the amount of traffic that will come my way. I need to make sure the aesthetics of the area are inviting, that people will feel good when pulling up to my spot, and have the space to park, and enjoy the evening.

Solution: It looks like I'm going to have to do my own location study too. I'm going to have to understand all the details about where I put my restaurant. I'll need to identify more than just the one location I have in mind. I should go out and select maybe up to a dozen locations, and then consider the pros and cons of each one. Clearly, I'm going to be doing a lot of reading, and a lot of writing.

Timing and the Plan: I need ample time to get this right. I'm going to define the timing appropriately to ensure all the details are considered.

Solution: As stated above I will detail my tasks lists. I will also put together an overall schedule. The task list will require several 3FE analyses on each subject. I will need to work on my business plan as well. I'll give myself a good year and half to complete the necessary research and develop an executable plan.

Food is my passion: I have a dozen signature recipes. I've been told I have a magic touch when it comes to food. I've never developed a menu. It's high time I tried.

Solution: I have to indulge my passion and practice it. I've been doing this for fun, now I need to make my fun a larger part of my life. To that end, I need to develop my menu, and practice it, again and again. After I put together the menu, I'll have some dinner parties and try it out. I won't tell the guests what I'm doing. I'll take notes, perfect my recipes, and put together a plan at the same time that will allow me to teach my secrets to others, so I don't spend all my time in the kitchen.

I need to see others that do it right: The truth is there are people out there that are successful for a reason. I have an approach to learning what they do, but it may extend my timeline. If that's the case, so be it.

Solution: I've worked in several different restaurants over the years before my career in Information Technology. However, I've spent so much time being an analyst that I think it would be a mistake to actually go out and try to do this without taking the time to re-learn how it's done and then learn from some of the best. To that end, I need to get a job working in a restaurant. I need to learn the secrets of some of the best see how they do it, and then do it for myself.

	The answer ... get a job.
Fundamentals	The Devil most assuredly lives in the details. And clearly, I have a veritable ton of details. I will not be successful at this at all without a clear and concise plan. I need one overarching plan that will be broken down into smaller plans. I can use the 3FE tool on each of those smaller objectives, putting together the executables that I will need at each level. This will take some time, but if I do it right. I CAN'T FAIL! Or rather, I won't face ultimate failure. I may fail, but it will be a manageable failure that I can learn from, and eventually reach success. I AM GOING TO 3FE THIS THING TO VICTRORY! **Task 1.** Develop my high-level task list. **Task 2.** Put together my initial funding plan **Task 3.** Develop my team. Who can I rely on for real help? **Task 4.** Put together research topic task list. **Task 5. Get a job at a high performing local restaurant!**
Execute	READY ... SET... EXECUTE!

The above is an initial analysis for opening a restaurant. There are those people out there who have an innate talent for glossing over the details, knowing where to fill in those details when they aren't listed, and executing effectively with only half a plan. Most of us are not like these people. We need a plan. We need the details written down. If we don't write the details down, we'll miss them, and depending on what the details are, it could lead to catastrophic effects for our little personal project. Remember, that damn devil lives in those details. You have to ferret him out and address him accordingly. I know I'm that kind of person, the kind who will gloss over the details, which is why I make use of the tool.

Let's break this down with regard to a franchise restaurant outside of our simple rectangles. Let's start with an understanding of the 2 rules of 3. Then, let's look at the high-level approach for reaching our objective. Finally, let's break down the tool for motivational empowerment as we try to view this opportunity of opening a restaurant in the most simplistic fashion we can manage.

Now, what are the 2 Rules of 3 again?

- 3FE

    - **The Methodology of Motivational Empowerment**
    - **Find, Focus, establish the Fundamentals, Execute**

- 3PoP

    - **The Principles of Prosperity (Real Estate, The Capital Markets, Entrepreneurship)**

How are we to utilize the tool?

3FE
The High Level Approach

Find : State the issue, problem, or opportunity
Focus : Write down the facts, 5WH
establish the Fundamentals : Possible Solutions
Execute : Run and Gun it! Follow the plan!

Let's break this opportunity down:

THE FIRST STEP IS **FIND:**
- FIND (Problem, Issue, Opportunity)
  - I want to open a restaurant!

THE SECOND STEP IS **FOCUS:**
- FOCUS (5WH)
  - What: A restaurant/franchise (Ice Cream, Burgers, THE SOUTH'S HOTTEST RESTAURANT?)
  - Who: Me, my potential customers, my investors
  - When: 6 months? 1 year? 2 years?
  - Where: Southside Metro Area? Northern Expansion?
  - Why: To build wealth and satisfy my passion!
  - How: Build a schedule (a plan) with appropriate detail.

THE THIRDS STEP IS Establish The

FUNDAMENTALS:

- What's the **PLAN?**
  1. Organize the franchise material you've gathered.
  2. Rank the franchise opportunities.
  3. Do another round of analysis on the franchise opportunities.
  4. Pro/Con analysis of opportunities.
  5. Organize and refocus for action your financial requirements.
  6. Organize personal financial assessment in-line with franchise requirements.
  7. Turn all this information into actionable **STEPS!**

THE LAST STEP IS **EXECUTE:**
- **EXECUTE!** Pull the trigger, and execute your plan!

The path is not so clear, but the approach is. Utilizing the tool may still feel complex, but feeling and actuality are not necessarily always the same thing. The point is if you have a dream, if you have a passion, if you are driven, then you absolutely must try. And if you are willing to try, make use of each and every tool available at your disposal in order to follow this passion. Make complete and total use of the tool for motivational empowerment and seize your dream. Take hold of it, no matter how big it seems, and start breaking it apart. Draw those rectangles and start working on your analysis.

So, are you going to open a franchise? Is it going to be a pizza joint? Does your heart move for hamburgers? Do you see the best sandwich shop on the west coast as your future dream endeavor? Maybe your future has a coffee shop in it, is that it? Are you really going to open the hottest soul food restaurant/café in the south? Or, do you have a plan to purchase rental homes as part of your commitment to the second principle of 3POP, and from there dive into the third principle by getting involved in home renovation, and eventually construction? Consider it. Do you really want to open your own spot? Do you have the perfect idea for the perfect invention, and need perhaps not a perfected plan, but a plan that will lead you to eventual, essential critical success? Are you ready? Do you have the requisite level of commitment to accompany your passion and desire? If so, then leverage this 3rd principle in the 2nd Rule of 3 by effectively utilizing the 1st. Make 3FE your tool of choice, consider all the options critically. Be motivated by your actions, and pursue your objective. If it's for you, then by all that's good pursue it with gusto! Give it everything you've got, blood, sweat, and tears. Use the tool. Become a successful entrepreneur by way of 3FE.

Chapter 8

3FE In Faith & Religion

We're entering into serious territory. Many would disagree with what I'm attempting to do here. However, there is a purpose in pursuing this path. My whole approach with regard to the simplification of critical thinking and the application of critical thinking in our everyday lives requires that we have a frank discussion on how critical thinking can be applied to everything we do.

There are of course levels of rigor in critical thinking, as it is so with just about everything else we do. In terms of the proper application of the Socratic-method or the in-depth study of philosophy and logic, critical thinkers delve deeply into the deep-end of thought, and add layers of complexity that might very well stagger the mind of the ordinary everyday individual (I stagger all the time).

As such, within the many layers of this complexity delineating common man from so-called and often self-ascribed uncommon or academic man, many perceive an implied line of demarcation. Sincere intelligence is on one side of the line. Common cognition is on the other. The mundanes have no right or hold on real thinking. Such pursuits are fit only for the intellectual. There is a line, both real, and one perceived. Therefore only a true intellectual can even begin to grasp the knowledge and fathom the deep understanding of the line as it cuts across the fabric of our society. In truth, from this perspective, faith exists on one side of this line. Science, logic, matters secular, and yes critical thinking and its application are perceived to be on the other side of this line.

I'm here to tell you, none of this is true. NONE OF IT!

What is the truth? The truth is that as we have worked assiduously throughout this book and others to provide tools to motivate and utilize critical thinking skills, one thing becomes abundantly clear. It is without equivocation possible, and as we evolve absolutely necessary, that we use the gifts we've been provided to THINK well. No matter the subject, no matter the issue or opportunity, no matter the span of time required to reach a conclusion or opinion, THINKING well is an absolute requisite, and critical thinking is the function directly defining thinking well.

This does not mean disavow yourselves of emotion. This does not mean let go of your passion. This does not mean seek to become a cold heartless automaton. This does not mean evolve into a Vulcan like Mr. Spock of Star Trek fame. No, all this means is that even in the heat of passion, in the throes of emotional turmoil, ups and downs, we have been blessed with the ability to take hold of our rampant emotions, and reason. It is still a worthwhile exercise if we reason after the fact, so long as the action we undertook while in the throes of passion was not a heinous one.

We are only human.

As humans we have always wrestled with the mystery of faith. It looms large in our being. There is faith in nothing. There is faith in everything. There is also faith in something particular. We have as human beings steeped in imagination and dogma built rules and regulations around much of our faith, given it credence and righteousness through historical events that speak to miracles and revelations. We take these events and with rules bound up within use them to govern the lives of men.

We humans when considering religion often discount that religion can simply be perceived as another form of government, a means of control. However, with the power of critical thinking, we can blast away the filters of perception and see the truth; and decide for ourselves what so many who sit in the high halls of religious power would deny the masses, even as they proselytize, to them their God given right, rife with arrogance and hypocrisy. Through the utilization of critical thinking skills, even in the greatest of societies, we imbue ourselves with the power to choose. We can proclaim the mystery of faith ... for ourselves.

Please, indulge me in this chapter on our humanity, and allow me to explain.

There is a special value placed on faith. When you consider it, you find it is a deep, soul-stirring concept. You can have faith without religion. You can have faith without a belief in a deity. Faith is a powerful human construct that describes the hope, desires, feelings we express within the confines of our humanity. Faith exists within the expansive freedom of a metaphorical vacuum. It needs no support. It is independent, and thrives without facts, or any kind of scientific basis whatsoever. I think that's part of its beauty.

You have faith when you believe in a thing. You have faith when you know deep down in your soul that the crooked ways will be made straight, and the barriers brought down. You have faith when you're lost, and without options, no possibilities, but for a small stirring in the pit of your stomach, a stirring that burns bright, and makes you believe that hope remains, and that you will be found. Faith tells you to never fear, you are not alone, even when you appear to be completely abandoned. These feelings, these thoughts, these deep-rooted beliefs have girded humankind through all the millennia of our long climb out of darkness. Even as we now create our light ourselves, we sometimes find it is not enough, and reserve belief for light that burns brightly clear to the soul, and nurtures without the burn of its brightness.

The mystery of faith has ever been the purview of the mystics, the spiritualists, the theologians. Humanity wrestles with the need to understand this mystery even as it has always drawn strength from it. It exists. It is real. All it requires is that you believe. This expression of belief has been pondered, studied, written about, illuminated in so many ways as to be beyond description. It is the basis of religion. And in religion we find the multitude of human expression, the believed explanation of the infinite, and acknowledgment of the finite, and our place within it.

Question everything.

There is a reason I ask you to do this, and it ties directly to the word I used in the previous paragraph, illuminated. What is illumination? And please don't get upset, angry, or in the opposite salivating or excited at the thought of world conspiracy and power-mongers. I don't indulge in that stuff and find it stands far outside the realm of critical thinking. I mean illumination with regard to its denotation, which is to enlighten, as with knowledge.

Humankind has long expressed and generated faith. Humankind has also long accepted and obeyed a given religion. Religion has brought fear, death, and intellectual darkness. Religion has also brought courage, joy, life, and intellectual enlightenment. It has existed in a dichotomy even as it has bound itself with faith. There have been times when one could not question religion, on pain of death. However, thankfully this is not one of those times … at least not in America … yet … may it always be so.

Question everything.

C.S. Lewis was an atheist. Yes, he was an atheist. The creator of the Lion, the Witch, and The Wardrobe did not believe in God. He saw no reason to place his faith in a capricious otherworldly deity who sat in judgment of us all. Know, there is only the here, the now, and the results of our expression. God is dead. He never lived.

You C.S. Lewis fans … upset yet?

Please, don't be. I'm making a point. C.S. Lewis was an incredible author, and most certainly in my opinion a powerful critical thinker. He questioned. He reasoned. In time, he arrived at a new revelation that changed his life. God is real, and the very essence of that reality is grounded in the religion called Christianity. Lewis had a crisis, a crisis of existence, a crisis of faith, and as he questioned all around him, he arrived through reasoning at the truth for himself.

As an aspiring critical thinker I believe in education, seeking knowledge, and applying the rigor of logic and reason to everyday issues and concerns. This is why I consider leveraging critical thinking skills with regard to religion. Questioning, thinking deeply about things opens up an entire universe of possibilities.

Now, here's the rub for some.

Questioning, thinking, utilizing logic and historical facts as well as so-called myths or parables to arrive at a realization of truth regarding a belief system is tricky at best. It is my opinion that there are some truths divined through facts that are irrefutable. They stand on their own due to an objective approach, such as the utilization of the scientific method. However, for the lay person such a rigor may not be feasible. We're not all scientists, and wouldn't know where to begin. However, we can all question. We can all seek knowledge on some level. And in the questioning, and the seeking, on matters of faith, where truth can most certainly be subjective, the activity of applying 3FE can very well illuminate a result that so strongly resonates with the individual spirit as to be completely and totally irrefutable. At least, that is my personal opinion.

Understand that such an exercise, as a pursuit of the truth, is a personal thing. An aspiring critical thinker would live that truth, as it would help him or her grow. Their actions would speak to that personal truth. However, they would not be in the business of proselytizing, or seeking to convert masses wholesale in a grand effort to convert the heathen to the saved. The aspiring critical thinker would not use such words as apostate, infidel, or defiler. These words are rarely ever used as a fact of what someone is, but rather a tool to categorize and stigmatize. These words are used as weapons and add no credible value in a world that aspires to critical cognition.

Question everything.

It is highly possible that you may live your life as a powerful intellectual, much like C.S. Lewis, and arrive at a completely different understanding. You see, it's okay to be an atheist. It's okay to be an agnostic. Of course, many religious proponents will tell you it's not okay, but I'll be honest with you. They have not yet arrived, and they do not fully embrace, or even understand the power of critical thinking. Faith is a personal thing my friends. And religion as a function of faith needs to be a personal thing as well. If you look around you'll be amazed at just how many people these days are coming to understand this significant if yet simple truth. You have the power to have a personal relationship with Allah, God, Vishnu, or absolutely nothing at all. It is entirely up to you.

With that understanding, and as an aspiring critical thinker, it is incumbent upon you to seek knowledge, to seek understanding, to try and find what truly resonates with you and your faith, even if what resonates is a denial of all religion, as well as a belief in any supreme deity or deities. As humans seeking to ever grow we owe it to ourselves to undertake such a journey of self-exploration. It will nurture the critical thinking mind and expand your knowledge, and if you have faith, it will expand your soul.

So what might you consider? Taoism, Buddhism, Hinduism, Zoroastrianism, Judaism, Islam, Christianity, Wicca, Rastafarianism, Sikhism, Confucianism, Shinto, Jainism, Unitarian Universalism, Cao Dai, Bahai Faith, Tenrikyo, Seicho-no-le, Church of World Messianity, Cheondoism, Vodun, Yoruba, Ashanti, Druidism, Druze, Gnosticism, Gypsies, Deism, Scientology, Santeria, Satanism, The Creativity Movement, Lukumi, Macumba, Eckankar, Elian Gonzalez religious movement, Romani, Native American Spirituality, Mowahhidoon … or maybe, maybe through all this introspection and study, you come upon a new truth, a certain truth that resonates outside the framework of these other religions. Within the realm of the critical thinking mind we build no walls and close no doors to possibility. We simply apply the mind to said possibility, and question it for veracity. This too can be applied to a given religion, and within the study by the individual could very well give rise to something new.

And so, to the purpose of the book, the utilization of the tool for motivational empowerment, how does 3FE apply to this critical thinking exercise, let's break down the rectangles and give it a try.

Oh! First, let's consider before we begin, the complexities of religion are multi-fold, wide and varying, and have consumed the entire intellectual capacities of some the world's most learned women and men. The tool is to make things easy. The tool is used to take the daunting and make it manageable, even fun, but always motivating. Finding what resonates, what you like, what drives you forward in terms of faith, and through structured religion, can either be extremely difficult, or ... easy. Now, let's break down some rectangles and give it a try.

3FE	Find ... Focus ... establish the Fundamentals ... Execute!!! **WHERE GOES MY SPIRIT?**
Find	**Who:** I have been raised in one faith. It has been of benefit, but as my mind has expanded, I want to know more. I want to see more. I want to understand more. **What:** I have faith, but it does not resonate with what I have always known. What out there will answer the call of my heart and soul, as well as my mind? **Where**: It does not matter where. Everywhere I am is where I seek my answer. However, I think the greatest where can start ... at the library. Reading is fundamental. **When:** I don't want to spend a lifetime searching, even as I do believe I'll spend a happy lifetime learning. I want to learn over the coming year and hopefully find that which answers my call. **Why:** My heart does not sing. I want it sing. I want my faith to fill me up with song.

	How: It may be a new perspective on what I already know, or it may be something altogether different. However, I want to do what most people refuse to do, or simply don't know how to do. I will read about something different.
Focus	**I have been strong in my faith.** Over time my strength has remained strong, but recently I find my strength waning. I understand why. It's simple. I don't believe. I have not lost my belief in God. However, I have lost my belief in the structures my religion has put around God. I need to seek, and I need to find. I need to walk a path that others have tread, a journey of self-discovery and truth. I can be logical in this pursuit. • I can take a piece of paper and write down the world's religions. • I will let my spirit guide me and research that which calls to me. • I will dive deep and write down what I discover. • I will resolve to make sure I step away from the structure of my current religion, but commit to researching it deeper on my own. **Solution:** I am qualified to know my own truth. I firmly believe we were given the power of choice for a reason. By undertaking this activity of discovery, I choose. **What is my faith?** Over the years I have been exactly what my parents, my wider family, expected of me. I've been a good steward of the family faith. I have remained true, even when I doubted. But now, I don't want to doubt. I seek fulfillment, and what I have is not providing it.

Solution: In order to understand and realize my own personal truth I have to have the courage to step away from family and friends, and firmly commit to fulfilling myself. To seek that which will make my heart sing. I've been fretting over this for some time. Now, I have the courage to do what I must. I will not waiver. I will hear my heart sing.

Expressions of self and where to find it: The library and the computer will be where I undertake my journey. The power of the written word will grant me access to so much information.

Solution: As I learn I may reach out to others in these faiths and get their perspective on the various religions. I'll include a trip to the library at least three times a week. I'll have to put it on my daily To Do list. It must be a firm commitment on my part.

This year will be the year of seeking and introspection: I firmly believe that my spirit is eternal. I firmly believe in something. I simply question what I have been taught to believe. It does not all ring true. I'll spend the next year taking the time to seek answers to my questions.

Solution: Some would limit the search to just the confines of the religion to which they were born. I was blessed with a strong education, and a healthy desire to learn. I know there are thoughts, ideas, beliefs out there that offer so many different possibilities. I have been gifted with the power of choice. I choose to learn. To enlighten myself and seek understanding of faith through the beliefs of others. In this, I will gain a greater understanding of myself.

Fundamentals	There is no reason to make this complicated. I'll keep it very simple. I'll make a list of religions. I'll investigate them. That which speaks to me, I'll research thoroughly. If nothing speaks to me … that is a different question that will require another analysis. I'll embrace it if it comes to that. But I know it won't. My spirit hums. It wishes to sing. I will search for the right kind of music. That is my plan.
Execute	READY … SET … EXECUTE ON FAITH!

As in the other chapters, this is merely an example of the 3FE approach. The tool is designed to be tailored to your specific needs. This entire chapter is dedicated to the ability to choose. To use the tools at your disposal to choose, to leverage critical thinking skills using a sound methodology, and find answers that suit you, and help you move forward with your life.

Please bear in mind that I mean all this as a gateway. The gateway is open to freedom. True freedom. I did not add this to tell you what to do, how to think, or what to believe. I added this because I want you to truly see the possibilities. I want you to know that when we move from the secular to the spiritual that you need not leave your critical thinking minds behind. In fact, if you do engage upon such discovery you will find the most intelligent theologians have always embraced intellectualism. Belief, faith, and the structure of religion are not exclusive of intelligence, science, worldly matters of either the mind or the body.

In fact, the search for the sacred and a keen understanding of from where it derives is clearly understood to be the purview of the intelligent mind, the pursuit of mental excellence, a task that can only be undertaken by those that embrace the choice, and choose critical thinking.

Do you choose to seek the sacred? Will you delve deep into your personal spirituality? Faith and religion are invariably efforts by humankind to define meaning, to give purpose to our lives, and acknowledge a desired truth that must be firm as concrete and strong as steel because we say it must be, that our faith can reach beyond the gulf of knowledge into the mystery and know without equivocation that within the confines of this wide universe we are not alone, for there is purpose, and we are part of that purpose.

Recognize yourself as you grow in critical cognition. And as you seek personal fulfillment, remember the tool is available to help you in your pursuit.

Your religion, whatever it may be, or the absence of it, can be more fully understood if you apply the gift of your mind to the critical task of understanding. It will always open your eyes to truth. It will prevent you from falling sway to false prophets and pretenders, sycophants, and God-hustlers. The men of faith who pimp the Lord will have no effect on you or your personal prosperity. You will not burn books. You will not rail against Harry Potter, and declare it the devil's work before an international audience, putting your sad stupidity on display for all to see. It will protect you and prevent you from loss. Working on your faith, and building the factual context around what you do, or don't believe is a worthy pursuit of the aspiring critical thinker. Faith goes beyond rationality, but you may find comfort in knowing accurately the basis upon which your faith rests, which is why choosing to pursue a deeper understanding is truly a courageous thing for any woman or man, or child for that matter. Your mind is indeed a terrible thing to waste, and if you put it to use for faith, for religion, or the pursuit of its absence from your life, you will truly be well served. Consider it critically.

Chapter 9
Social 3FE

Find, Focus, establish the Fundamentals in your social interactions. We've gone so far as to consider it within the framework of our faith. Why not consider the perspective of applying it in other aspects of our everyday lives?

Let us consider the sci-fi life form mentioned in the previous chapter, the Vulcan from Star Trek: cold, logical, a mind that operates as a machine, suppressing all emotion because it interferes with the ability to reason at an optimal level, to achieve the utmost efficiency in mental processing. Would this be the end result if we embrace critical cognition and apply it to our social setting? Would we become cold automatons? And would we as logical beings that leverage a tool for critical thinking allow such a travesty to spread across the breadth of our lives, suffusing us with cold logic, never to embrace the heat of passion or the cold of despair and loss? Consider it critically. Yes, please do. Why? Because Star Trek is a television show. It is science-fiction fantasy, and even though we humans could discipline ourselves to behave in such a manner, why would we?

We are not our best as critical thinking logic machines that feign emotion and smile because it's what we're supposed to do, as opposed to openly displaying how we feel. No, in fact when figuring out what we want to do, what we want to be, how we want to be, in finding our true passion, the goal can only truly be realized and built upon when we human beings embrace our compassion, embrace all our emotions, our joys as well as our pains. In the elevation of self we become more effective critical thinkers, greater lovers of life, and each other, evolving both individually and socially. 3FE is but a tool to help facilitate this growth, not inhibit it. Consider, it is the tool for motivational empowerment, by its very function, it's designed to make you feel … good, even through the heated crucible of the challenge.

3FE	Find ... Focus ... establish the Fundamentals ... Execute!!! **Issue:**
Find	Identify the issue. Find what it is. Open your eyes, ready your mind, set your attitude to full on positive and engage in true critical thinking. Question everything, and then write it down. Who ... What ...Where ...When ...Why
Focus	Look closely at what you've found. Focus on it. These pieces of information aren't truly information yet. It's all just data. Dig into the details and clarify the bits and pieces of the data. Take note of the relationships between the bits of data. What additional details are there to consider?
Fundamentals	As the relationships between the data points becomes clear, a path arises from the data, and things begin to make sense. When data has meaning, it becomes information. Information has value, and inherently can lend itself to a solution. This is the Fundamentals, the essential tasks that bind the information together into action steps that resolve the issue.
Execute	Because sometimes you need an execution plan. Maybe you're going to execute in phases. Maybe you'll execute in one fell swoop, all at once. However, you do it, do it with emphasis! EXECUTE! EXECUTE! EXECUTE!

The rectangles are where the work takes place. The rectangles define the method, and inherent in the method is the mission. However, in our social settings we're not always looking for a mission. Invariably, we just want to live. The whole point around considering 3FE in social interactions is that we ensure that even as we tone it down, we never turn it completely off. The goal is to treat the mind like any other muscle. We want to work it to maximum proficiency. The need is there, and through mental rigor we exercise it. However, just like a finely honed muscle, even when it's relaxed, it's working remarkably well.

You should be able to enjoy interactions with friends, and as you discuss things together, points of conflict may arise. You should be able to think critically about what is being said in the midst of the conversation. Your emotions make take hold and you may run rampant, wildly gesticulating and exclaiming this that and the other, agreeing or vehemently disagreeing. But even as you do this, you must exercise your mind with the critical thinking rigor. You must be able to pull back, take a breath, and think about what is being said, and what you are saying.

This requires you to listen. Yes, listening is a critical thinking activity. You see, in far too many of our interactions we spend an inordinate amount of time just hearing the opening few words of what someone else is saying. The rest of the time we're thinking about what we're going to say as a response. So think about it. How can you truly be listening to what the other person is saying, when you're spending all your time thinking about what you're going to say back, before he or she has even finished speaking? Let me answer for you. You can't.

Either you do listen, or you don't. And as an aspiring critical thinker, it is an absolute must that you listen. As you listen, you must consider what was said. You must consider the other person's perspective. You must think about why you either agree, or disagree. You must consider what you will say in response.

As we've seen, the 3FE tool is the go-to instrument for the aspiring critical thinker. It breaks the complex into the simple. It allows you to take a breath and actually consider what it is you're actually doing, what you're contemplating, how you're acting. In social interactions we often bring our emotions to the fore and let them predominate.

Invariably we bring forth just *our* emotions alone. We give no consideration to the emotions of others, or the specific person we're engaging. Just as we're caught up in conflict at work we are also caught up in conflict at home. However, conflict in and of itself can be good or bad. We must strive for positive conflict and eschew negative conflict. In order to note when the conflict level is rising and our emotions are taking overriding control we must be able to think. We must be able to pause, and assess, and within this pause is where we may flex the muscle of our mind, trained in the rigors of critical cognition. We can bring our mind to the fore in order to better manage our emotions, and thereby improve the level of our engagement and the quality of our social interactions.

Consider your family.

Our families are far from perfect. They are the source of both joy and pain. You love. You laugh. You scream. You cry. You do all these things with family. They can lean on you, reminding you that blood is thicker than water. They can uplift you, or they can drag you down. The interactions with family can be absolutely toxic, if we let them. However, sometimes our filters or passion and responsibility for family prevent us from actually seeing what is real, from hearing what is truly said, from acknowledging the real truth of a given situation. In the break of the breath between moments, you can flex the muscles of your mind, and reach for 3FE.

Plain and simple: Find and list the details of your relationship. Focus on what is good, and what is bad, and what is either lifting you up, and supporting the necessity to remain connected, and what is actually bringing you down, if not downright destroying you to the core of your soul, and supporting the necessity to simply close the door on them, to never let it open again. Establish a Fundamental plan to do whatever needs to be done with the family. Finally, Execute it. Utilizing 3FE to empower yourself and motivate you to action within the confines of familial relationships can allow you to more readily evolve your true emotions, the positive ones, embrace your passions, think and realize a better reality for yourself, or/and those family members who are struggling along with you, perhaps in equal measure. You can all be better, together.

Consider your child.

I separate the critical thinking activity for a child from the family because you cannot, must not, ever consider shutting yourself off from your child. The consequences are almost always dire for both child and parent. Of course, the consequences always weigh heaviest on the child. You can't abandon a toxic child. You can choose to shut the door of your life on a child. If you put your child up for adoption the connection is always there. The child may be better off, but you will suffer within yourself. I promise you there is no other option in this, unless you're a psychopath or sociopath, and those categories of human experience must be reserved for an entirely different book.

A child is the purpose of all. I mean this sincerely. We procreate, we create material things in which to reside, and procreate. We leave what we create to what we procreate. However, we always, always lose sight of the pure purpose of procreation, and in the creation of life, in the creation of a child is the million trillion possibilities of the infinite. I won't take this any further. This book is about critical thinking, so in this I of course want you to think deeply about what I just mentioned. I want you to consider it. And from this I want you to always be of a mind to think deeply and lovingly about our children.

With that in mind we can look upon the world in which our kids live and apply the tool for motivational empowerment in the absolute most important way we can imagine, the betterment of the lives of our children. I want you to think about all that we've gone over in these pages. I want you to consider the approaches.

Consider the material, the rectangles themselves, and the critical questions that reside within them. I want you to think about the process of breaking the complex down into more manageable constituent components. I then want you to look at the children, and think about them.

We can use 3FE in order to gain a critical thinker's understanding of the problems facing our children, and define real-world solutions that will truly benefit them, and allow them to reach their maximum potential as individuals seeking to be the best of themselves within this world, grand stewards of a mental and physical well-being that readies them to take what we leave behind and not only live in it, but thrive in it, and make it far better.

No matter the problem, physical, emotional, mental, think critically upon the problem. Is it drugs? Is it child abuse? Is it abject poverty? Is it access to educational materials and opportunity? Is it rape and molestation? Is it criminal gang activity? Is it a love for television, the idiot box? Is it a love of clothes? Is it the worship of all things material? Is it an intense hate of reading? What is it? What is the problem? My friends, my people, look at the children. Grab pen and paper. And let us get to work. They are our children. There is no more important task before us.

People, the interactions between us can consume all of heart, mind, and soul. They can wear us down and quite literally break us down. They can catapult us into a slow malaise to eventual erosion and perhaps catatonia, or even self-destruction unto death.

It can be just that serious.

It is at just such times that you must be able to take a breath, grab hold of your emotions and truly consider things critically. It's not an easy thing at all. No, it can sometimes seem impossibly difficult. Of all the scenarios in which we may discuss utilizing 3FE and critical thinking the absolutely most challenging can be within the confines of our social interactions, the very personal relationships that bind us and define friends and family, and most certainly where children are concerned.

These interactions are the purview of our emotions. We rarely consider them areas in which we can think positively, or rationally, or rather when we do try to be rational it is used as an instrument of abuse, which can be far worse sometimes than a yell, a slap, or even a fist. It's not about the rational. It's about thinking, and perspective. It's about thinking, and understanding the emotion, not just your own, but the emotions of those with whom you interact.

Within the confines or our relationship, and our emotions, as aspiring critical thinkers it bears recalling and internalizing the hallmark of the critical thinker:

The aspiring critical thinker seeks to understand and internalize the perspective of others, most especially when that perspective is diametrically, or even violently opposed to your own.

At the heart of any issue, any situation, any problem, are the varying perspectives of the individuals involved, as well as the varying perspectives of the problem itself, which can lead to varying solutions, one of which may be far superior than all others. However, without perspective, without the benefit of critical thinking, you will never know, and therefore be unable to recognize and thereby execute this truth. You will have no action for your resolution. Remember, the path to wisdom and truth is brightly illuminated by the light of perspective.

Chapter 10

VOTING 3FE

Yesterday, I had a very sobering conversation with a good friend of mine. We were discussing politics, one of my many necessary interests, and he told me he was not going to vote in the upcoming election. I nodded my head and said I understood. He immediately began to elaborate the whys of his chosen action. We were at work and he mentioned how our organization had experienced some change and for an incredibly large part, that change had been incredibly good. In fact, we had experienced one of our most profitable quarters in all our company's storied history. This was a powerful testament to the men and women at the helm of our vast company.

However, for him things had not changed at all. He said America had not gotten any better, and they had not gotten any worse. In his opinion things were only going to get worse, America was on the downtrend, and his reasoning was the larger majority of the people that controlled things didn't want to give intelligence a chance. He said people liked the gut. They liked popularity. He said people were bound and determined to elect stupid people to high office because smart people that controlled stupid people were good at helping stupid people control the masses, by funding powerful messages that the regular masses sopped up like so much candy.

He said people didn't want change that they could believe in, that was hard fought and came at a high price. He said people wanted the surface, the cheap and the quick, and that which sounded good, and felt good. In that, he said the mass majority of the people were on crack, and they would negate his vote … so why bother.

I sat there in silence for a moment, flabbergasted by his clear unassailable logic.

He shrugged and said, "That's just the way it is, bro. That's how the world works. I'm not wasting my time on that bull."

I took a deep breath, and said, "That ... is the biggest mound of bullshit I have ever heard!"

Okay, I've been working on my cursing and I really didn't say this. Still, I'll freely admit I love to use a good expletive on occasion. In this instance what I said was, "Well, I hear you my brother. I hear you. But let me just ask you pointedly, do you really think you matter so little?"

The way I said it, in measured tones with due consideration and a very discerning eye focused on his eye, made him take pause. As we are both educated men, I didn't need to elaborate, but I chose to do so anyway, just to bring the point home.

"You know I'm all about critical thinking, respect, and a desire to live in a more holistic, better world. My brother, you've heard how a butterfly's wings can precipitate a hurricane on the other side of the world, the butterfly effect. I tell you everything matters. Every movement matters. Every gesture, every action, and most importantly every vote matters.

You know too many American's still don't vote. There are powers afoot now to limit that number even more, all a part of an ideologically driven power agenda that would seek to create an oligarchical empire with us as cogs, gears in the machine with no voice, no opportunity. Our forebears died for the right to vote. You do them tremendous disrespect when you choose to do otherwise. All Descendants of the Emancipated have an obligation, a duty to exercise the franchise, we the Descended as well as every last citizen of this nation. There can be, and is no choice, not if you would respect everything that we struggled for, fought for, died for.

And we, as leaders in our communities, in our nation, beyond the boundaries of ethnicity have an obligation to the lead the way, to show them a better way, to explain to them that they do matter. Each vote is a strike against consolidated power. Each vote is a voice that speaks for all the people, not just some of the people. Each vote let's the world know that you exist, that you matter, that you care, that you are engaged. And it can't stop there, not just one time my brother, not just one election. No, you must do better. You must aspire to be better. You must remain engaged. Act in all the elections, not just the big ones. This is our life. This is our future. This brave new interconnected world, and the social networking phenomenon has contributed to Arab Spring, has contributed to bringing down sick politicians who lie to the people of their state as well as their families so they can fly off to another country and party.

We can hold those in power to a higher regard. We can make them be accountable. We can show them we count. We can be leaders as well, guiding those who we elect to lead, reminding them that they work at our behest for us, not over us. By doing this we realize the change in our world we so readily seek. Now, are you going to vote? Are you going to vote? Your vote counts. You can and do make things change. Will you vote?"

The answer was yes.

We went on to discuss exactly how we should vote, and how we should get engaged. There was more sharing of knowledge along those lines. It was an absolutely wonderful discussion, one I would readily have again anywhere with anyone. There is power in the franchise. Voting is one of the most powerful things you can do as a citizen of a given nation. To choose to not vote is to abdicate your power, your authority, your will, your right to others. You are in essence signing over your life to someone else, for in the aggregate your individual power can and does bend power in the aggregate, thereby dictating policy. In our modern world of ever-ready communication it will command policy even more. You must choose to be engaged.

So to the point, why do I include voting in this book? Why write a chapter on the application of critical thinking skills with regard to how we vote, and how we can leverage the tool for motivational empowerment in this activity?

To make it simple, this book is not just about critical thinking in school. Kids can't vote. However, it behooves them to be prepared and ready to understand the importance of the activity. This book is not just about critical thinking on the job. However, your positive engagement in political activity can have a direct bearing on the policies and procedures your job institutes, thereby affecting your day-to-day work life. This book is not just about critical thinking as you pursue your entrepreneurial dreams. However, your engagement in the political process can directly determine the economic environment that prevails as you try to start your business. This book is not just about social interactions and religion with regard to critical thinking skills. However, your utilization of such skills can help improve your interactions greatly. This book is not just about using critical thinking skills when you vote. However, the very real truth is that when it comes to the power of the franchise, using critical thinking skills is ABSOLUTELY MANDATORY. This book is about all those things and more. It is about the utilization of critical thinking skills in all the varied facets of our lives, with the desire to make our lives much better.

Understand, we can't afford to vote for someone because they look good. We can't afford to vote for someone because they speak well. We can't afford to vote for someone because they seem like the kind of person you could sit down and have a beer with. No, the vote is far too important for such trivialities. It is high time the people of today took voting as seriously as those who died for it in the past. It is time that we not only voted, but voted with accountability, and hold those who we elect to positions of power accountable. We can only do this through the full utilization of our intellects, our ability to reason and discern, and the tool for motivational empowerment can make this activity that much easier.

When I vote I utilize 3FE in order to understand the clear facts around my candidate, and I relate those facts to the things I think are important to me personally. I start with my personal needs, wants, and desires. Then, I consider what this candidate is offering with regard to my family. Then, I raise my perspective a level and try to think about what his policies mean for my community, my state, and if applicable my nation. As an aspiring critical thinker I even try to take the time to consider what this one woman or man may mean to the world, and how his or her actions may impact the world.

Understand clearly, one person's actions can and sometimes does impact the entire planet. This is not an opinion, but a fact. Such consideration is required because that is just how powerful the American franchise truly is. Your one vote is just one vote. But the word *just* is wholly inappropriate. Your one vote matters. It counts for something. Your votes represent your perspective, your opinion on how things should be, through the power of the ballot. When taken into consideration in the aggregate your vote, your actions, translated through the power of the policies implemented by your Mayor, Alderman, Congressman, Senator, Judges, and President clearly have an impact on the entire world, such is the power of the ballot.

You must vote. I say again, you must vote. Your nation needs you to vote. However, as we understand how important the franchise is we must consider critically what is required to make your vote useful. An electorate that votes based on the dole, what the government can give them and nothing more is a vote we don't need. An electorate that votes based on ideology and the propaganda that has injected mighty opinions dressed up as filtered flop-sided facts into the mind is a vote we don't need. An electorate inundated by our information rich culture, rife with the meme viral poison of MDC (Media-Driven ConsumerCelebreality) is quite clearly, a vote we don't need. Yes, we need our nation voting. We need our entire nation voting. We need all our people to participate. But more importantly, we need them to be educated, informed, discerning participants. We need people to vote, after they have given the candidates due consideration. We need people to think. We need them to think critically.

The application of the critical thinker's approach is simple. Study the candidates. Study the issues. However, due to the ideological deluge of political partisanship, the total inundation of Left versus Right versus Center, far too many of us ... no, almost the entire population of us that even take the time to vote, don't stop to think. We don't stop to consider.

Our emotions cannot be denied, however we must learn to keep them in check. As constituents, as participants in our political system we owe it to ourselves, and the candidates who endeavor to do good works, to take the time to study what's happening around us and to us. We need to take the time to conduct personal research into the issues and the candidates that claim they can address them. We also must approach the issues with clear and resolute reasoning disavowed of emotion and rhetoric, so we can readily identify those ineligible candidates that get into politics to secure a position of power for personal gain at the expense of the people, those who are highly corruptible, and will do NO good works, because they truly don't care.

The educating of the masses with the mandate to apply critical thinking with regard to the voting process is clearly a must. Without such focus, without the benefit of education, we fail in the process of moving forward as a nation efficiently. We fail in the process of elevating our politics. Yes, voting right now for far too many is not about an education. However, we must commit now that education is a must, a requisite for effective voting. This does not mean that we ban people from the polls. What it means is that each of us who does vote makes education disavowed of ideology a personal responsibility, and that we not only take it upon ourselves to vote with an educated mind and a critical thinking approach, but that we spread this good news of voting with a critical thinking mind by being good examples, and sharing our personal experiences, just as I'm about to do now.

I had initially been remiss, what with all the drama unfolding at the national level. I had attended a health care rally at North Gwinnett High School were John Linder and Tom Price railed against ObamaCare, something I had taken the time to investigate myself, even as some law makers proudly proclaimed they would not even take the time to read the legislation. I'm a strong supporter of Obamacare because I read the bill and the law, and worked to understand the law's facts, and its implications. I don't have it all. I'm not all that smart. But the point is to try, to seek your understanding, to engage in policy making and make your vote matter of your own accord. Oh, I also call it Obamacare because like the GOP I'm a strong proponent of word usage and laying claim to meaning. The President's team already knew what the GOP was doing with word possession, but they chose to not go that route. Why, I'm not sure. Affordable Care Act is so boring, and hedging to not tie the President's name to the law really didn't work that well at all.

However, the local race was beckoning and I was not even aware of the options. I had options! How wonderful! Oh, I knew John Linder was serving his last term in office. I also knew he had a hand picked successor. I had already started to see the signs of radical extremism from the Republican contenders vying for the 7th seat. Now please understand, I support radicalism when appropriate, and I like getting extreme. I find it asinine in the extreme to take such words and provide them with narrow constrained definitions indicative of painful vitriolic hate-filled ideology. However, that's beside the point. As I was saying, I was pleased to find I had options. It was time to start Focusing. However, first I would have to Find all the requisite details. The devil lives in the details as we all know. A decision, any decision, must be considered critically, and requires facts, not filtered facts, not shaded facts, not facts refracted through ideological filters that bend and twist facts into opinions that resemble facts.

No, just the facts.

My candidate of choice was clear from the moment I ran across his information on Facebook. He appeared to have a late start. Nothing against my candidate, it's just that during the time in question he was still serving our country in the military and had not yet got his ground machine running in order to get the message out. Over a few short weeks that changed. Utilizing my mental tool for motivational empowerment 3FE: Find, Focus, establish the Fundamentals, and Execute, I dove in deep.

My candidate's name was Doug Heckman. Here's what I did.

3FE	**Find ... Focus ... establish the Fundamentals ... Execute!!!** **Choosing a Candidate For United States Congress in Georgia's 7Th Congressional District**
Find	**Who:** I needed to choose a candidate • Rob Woodall, John Linder's chosen successor • Jody Hice, • Doug Heckman **What:** The 7th District Congressional Seat. The platform material of each candidate. What are their positions on the issues and what have they stated they will do in order to solve those issues? **Where:** The entire country, but first due consideration must be made for my local community. The old saying is all politics is local, right? **When:** The election is approaching. It's time to conduct research and consider what each candidate is bringing to the table. **Why:** Simply put, I must live what I espouse. I have been doing this for a few years now, and it has become my standard approach to voting. I have to truly consider the candidates not on something empty and simple, but consider them based on facts, and what they state on PAPER to be their objectives.

	How: Simple, which is why such an important task need not be either trivialized or considered intractable. Reading is fundamental. All I have to do is read, and consider the options. After reading, how will their positions affect me personally, then affect my family, then my wider family, then my community, then my city, state, nation, the planet. Take it to its logical conclusion.
Focus	**Doug Heckman** The candidate's name is Doug Heckman. He didn't post his party affiliation initially, a negative according to some. To me, this was uplifting. Given the tenor of the times he was being tactical, a soldier taking appropriate action. In the heightened atmosphere of anger and apathy he demanded we focus on Doug Heckman the man, and what he stood for, not his party affiliation. It's not like he could keep it a secret anyway, nor would he. He just wanted the initial information to reflect his many facets, who he was, and what his stance was on the issues. **Additional Perspective** To be balanced and in keeping with my mandate as an aspiring critical thinker I remain true to the hallmark of the critical thinker, namely the sincere ability to internalize and truly seek to understand the perspective of others, most especially when those perspectives are diametrically, even violently opposed to your own. With that understanding I consider the other candidates, in particular Jody Hice and Rob Woodall, Linder's chosen successor. I find both of them coming up way short in my own personal opinion, which I am entitled to. However, it is not because they are Republicans. I've voted GOP before, and hope to be able to do so again.

No one party should take your vote for granted. The exercise must always be *understanding the facts*, getting a sincere education on the issues and candidates. One must determine if the candidate's perspective falls in line with your own perspective and what you want and need from an official in order to achieve critical success for yourself, your family, your community, your nation.

Jody Hice

Jody Hice, a vitriolic ideologue, heat and brimstone pastor is someone I clearly understand. He's one of many … all of them backward. He posted a sign on a billboard next to Interstate-85 that asked if you "HAD ENOUGH OF OBAMA'S CHANGE." It had the Soviet hammer and sickle placed over the C in Change. This was distasteful not because I support our President, but rather because it was just distasteful and divisive in general. Jody is clearly not a critical thinker. As I stated he is an ideologue, a partisan avatar of divisiveness that prefers the heated violence of words that cause pain and suffering, pushing us farther apart instead of striving to bring us closer together. I can never vote for such a man. Hate is not a valued commodity.

Rob Woodall

Rob Woodall is a far better candidate than Jody Hice. Still, looking at the details I can tell we are miles apart in perspective.

I see him holding fast to partisan politics, policies I simply do not find agreeable or forward thinking, and will not help me personally. He does not appear to be considerate of the issues on a higher level indicative of strong critical thinking skills (remember the hallmark – the current GOP position in total is all about power and winning, ideology and scorched-earth positions …

makes no sense), though he is far superior to Jody Hice, I still find Mr. Woodall wanting.

He cannot be my candidate. I can probably have a beer with the man though.

Additional On Doug

Doug Heckman eventually posted his own billboard sign on I-85. It showed him in his combat fatigues, as an Army Colonel who served with distinction in Iraq. At the top instead of asking if you were tired of change, it asked, "HAD ENOUGH OF PARTISAN POLITICS?" Here was a candidate that echoed my own mind and personal goal for all our people deeply involved in the need for a good political process. ELEVATE OUR POLITICS!!! We must close the ideological divide. We must come together. Doug Heckman believes in this. In fact, in studying him closer the only place we seemed to diverge was support for that conservative jewel, the Fair Tax. I support the Fair Tax, but as an aspiring critical thinker I also fervently support the process of compromise, pro-and-con, deeper analysis from varying perspectives in order to define a more cohesive solution. Doug supports a different approach, but fully embraces the need for tax reform. This disparity in our views on approach only gave us something good to engage in critically, as I imagined us sparing mentally in my mind.

However, what was even more pleasing was talking to him personally and realizing that he was indeed an aspiring critical thinker who made it his business to know the facts, that he would indeed strive to be a strong advocate for ALL the people of Georgia's 7th district and represent our perspectives with honor and distinction. I was already ahead, thinking I had found my candidate.

In keeping with the 3FE methodology I'll take the time to focus on the information I've collected regarding my candidates by going to their sites and printing their platforms.

The utilization of the web provides us with unprecedented access to information. Unfortunately the deluge of information has created a glut of nonsense, static that can cloud the pursuit of facts. Critical thinking skills inoculates one against the preponderance of the inane. Even as I use the tool I must remember to consider the hallmark of the critical thinker, and always question the source. Take nothing for granted. It's easy to be manipulated. Words are power, and ideas form ideology. Remain wary, and mentally alert.

I use the information provided by the candidates themselves to determine how they might approach problem solving in the United States Congress. I'll pull in much more data than I have listed here. I'll even pull in the opinions of the pundits, the ideological and even the inane. This will provide … perspective.

The litmus test is whether or not their perspectives adhere to what I personally believe to be the best way to solve the problems facing our country, not what some pundit tries to tell me. I must discern how his policies would impact me directly.

In the final summation as I focused on the details I can clearly see that Doug would seek to be a real problem solver, leaning into positive conflict in order to determine the best path forward, taking into consideration the perspectives of all those involved in the debate, and all those impacted. I perceived he would do this to the best of his ability, and by making this determination I quickly determined a course of action for me personally.

Fundamentals	The plan is simple. In an effort to be engaged in the political process, to be a positive voice for change, I'll get active. 1. Meet Doug and discuss the issues. Is he open? Will he listen to his possible future constituent? 2. If the meeting is as favorable as the information I've read, help the man out. 3. Pick up signage and post it in the community. 4. Tell others in the community what kind of man Doug Heckman presents as a candidate for office. 5. Blog and Vlog in support of Doug. 6. Explain why you personally believe he will be the best choice to serve Georgia's 7th District. 7. Vote early, get it in where you fit in.
Execute	With my plan in hand, and my approach for supporting and promoting my candidate, there is only one thing left to do. EXECUTE! Pull the trigger, run and gun it!

Okay, I guess one might say I've gone too far. Some might want to write off this entire chapter. I do understand. I allowed my recent political choices to be aired publically, thereby perhaps filtering the information I'm seeking to convey to the reader. I hope that is not the case, and it if is allow me to clarify so I can make plain what I am honestly attempting to do here.

Traditionally, people of the world are not positively politically active. Oh they're active to some degree, all the way from not at all to actually running for office, to running up and down the street with bats, pitchforks, the fire and the flame, most notably to protest some political action ... by burning down their own neighborhoods.

See, no critical thinking skills.

However, we have entered into a new era of participation and engagement. As I've said, never before have we had such access, such availability of information, such powerful communication. We are truly in the midst of a paradigm shift, and the old perspectives cannot be allowed to persist. I think this chapter is important because as I seek to teach critical thinking skills in our everyday lives, and the harnessing of the tool for motivational empowerment, it becomes plainly evident that we cannot sit idly by and allow power to coalesce and operate around us as though we are not involved. The world is changing and growing, and we may choose to be a peasant, or an isolationists, but existing, or subsisting in an effort to not impact the world, won't preclude the world from impacting you ... on a personal level.

With this consideration as we seek to grow as critical thinkers 360 degrees 24/7 360 days of the year, or rather continue to aspire to be critical thinkers of a high caliber, we absolutely must leverage the tool in our process of voting, of engaging in the political process. I firmly believe we absolutely must ELEVATE OUR POLITICS. We must leave the old way of things behind. We must believe in CHANGE. But clearly, we must all learn to see the truth if we are to elevate our politics.

We must inoculate ourselves from the power of MDC (Media-Driven ConsumerCelebreality) which ideologues wield as the ultimate weapon of power and control. Propaganda, heated rhetoric, words that stir the passion of the soul and freeze the mind are commonplace. Words that make us jump up and yell things like, "But he's a Muslim!" Or, "Put 'em all on a bus and ship 'em back to Mexico!" Or, "They are simply too stupid to see the light, it's either our way or no way. I don't care, I'll let it all burn down."

This is the state of our politics. The ideological divide is wide and with the rise of President Obama it got even wider and has rising to an apex under President Trump. We must see what happens under President Biden. People have always chosen their camps, their teams, their causes to support. However, in a time when we seem to have lost the ability to listen and understand, when compassion is a bad word, and compromise is evil, critical thinkers must come to the forefront. Critical thinkers must claim their place at the head of the table, because only aspiring critical thinkers clear the air of all the noise and nonsense. Only critical thinkers could pierce the cloud of groundless logic that is truly illogic, and filtered facts dressed up as the truth. Only critical thinkers can look at spin, and see it for what it is, and not be swayed. Critical thinkers can compromise, for the good of us all. They can leverage the tool for motivational empowerment to breakdown those complex ideas of ideology and belief. They can cut through to the core of the matter and discern the truth with its many facets. They can take that which will benefit us all and utilize it to maximum effectiveness.

Each of you must be a leader. You must become a critical thinker in your own right. You must demand that we elevate our politics, as the social contracts we bind each other with, the culture that we create, impacts all our lives. We must learn to live with each other, and love each other beyond mere tolerance. We must embrace each other with the compassion and love that we know we can realize for each other, caring for the well-being of us all, no matter our ethnicity, creed, color, or religion. We must each of us be a leader, and demand that those that lead us in the aggregate be aspiring critical thinkers.

Non-thinkers need not apply, simply because they are not qualified. We must each of us embrace the tool for motivational empowerment and utilize 3FE to gird ourselves for tomorrow's challenges with a honed mind ready to engage with maximum effectiveness, and the need and desire to succeed. We must seek each other out, motivate others, and be seen in the doing, so that the word will spread the world over, and we can one day realize a better day when we all vote, are all engaged, and are all committed to a better life for each other, ourselves, and our posterity. Consider it critically.

Closing

Now, after the last chapter. I hope I haven't lost some of you. I must say this because the political climate is so acrimonious. I don't want all that we've covered to get lost in the noise created by ideologues that have suffused your mind. Please take a deep breath, step back, and look at this holistically. Again, I state my purpose in this book, in this passionate mission, is to not just affect change at work, but at home, and in the spaces in between. I truly wish to have you embrace a mental tool that can ease your life journey, or even make it more challenging, as you become more motivated to take on challenges you never thought you could face before embracing critical thinking skills.

Truly use critical thinking skills to divest yourself of ideology, of party, of team, of all the things that influence you completely, without giving you the benefit of deciding for yourself. Your power to choose is always ever-present. However, the power of MDC, the meme disease that bleaches the mind, robs you of your will to choose, your ability to choose of your own accord. It allows others to choose for you. There is only one inoculant, critical thinking skills. And there is a simple tool that can aid you in embracing critical cognition, can aid you in utilizing critical thinking skills, and allow you to stand immune to the corrosive effects of Media-Driven ConsumerCelebreality, whether it be used to inject your mind with a political message, or make you go buy materialistic things you know you can't afford, and really don't need, but have been made to believe that you truly want. The tool for motivational empowerment will allow you to face these daily challenges, and stand immune.

3FE will excite you. It will allow you to find your long buried desire, embrace your passion, look upon books with real curiosity.

Yes, you will read. You will come to love books, because you will understand that books, not the idiot-box, is the food of the critical thinking mind. You will seek to expand your horizons. You will desire opportunity. You will seek to find the boots that were made specifically for you. You will seek them out, and when you find them, you will put them on with confidence, secure in the knowledge that with these boots on your feet you walk into a new day, a new day of unknown challenges that may vex you, even bring you to failure, but you won't fear, for you are armed with the tool for motivational empowerment, and you will feel empowered to reach down and grab the straps of those boots, and with pure, intense enthusiasm, due as so many demand … you will lift yourself up by your own bootstraps.

3FE	Find ... Focus ... establish the Fundamentals ... Execute!!! **I have ... an opportunity**
Find	Identify the issue. Find what it is. Open your eyes, ready your mind, set your attitude to full on positive and engage in true critical thinking. Question everything, and then write it down. Who ... What ...Where ...When ...Why
Focus	Look closely at what you've found. Focus on it. These pieces of information aren't truly information yet. It's all just data. Dig into the details and clarify the bits and pieces of the data. Take note of the relationships between the bits of data. What additional details are there to consider?
Fundamentals	As the relationships between the data points becomes clear, a path arises from the data, and things begin to make sense. When data has meaning, it becomes information. Information has value, and inherently can lend itself to a solution. This is the Fundamentals, the essential tasks that bind the information together into action steps that resolve the issue.
Execute	Because sometimes you need an execution plan. Maybe you're going to execute in phases. Maybe you'll execute in one fell swoop, all at once. However, you do it, do it with emphasis! EXECUTE! EXECUTE! EXECUTE!

USE THE TOOL TODAY!

www.ingramcontent.com/pod-product-compliance
Lightning Source LLC
Chambersburg PA
CBHW020421220526
45464CB00002B/515